On

Therapy

Written by Paula Reed BSc (Hons) MBPsS

with

Steven Johns MA – The Writers' Coach

Edited by Mary Johns

Front Cover Illustration by Ian Ward

Graphic Design by Alison Poole Designs Ltd

Paula Reed's Onion Therapy

www.oniontherapy.co.uk

This first edition published 5th May 2019
by
Paula Reed
24 Branston Road
Barrow on Soar
Loughborough
Leicestershire
LE12 8XI

Email: info@oniontherapy.co.uk

www.oniontherapy.co.uk

All transcript, formatted material, artwork and photographs
© 2019 Paula Reed and Steven Johns
Except for:

Front cover illustration and artwork
© Ian Ward
38 Halstead Close, Forest Town, Mansfield Nottinghamshire NG19 0RR
www.ianrward.co.uk

Graphic Design by Alison Poole Designs Limited
10 Priory Drive, Stainton, Middlesbrough TS8 9AW
www.alisonpooledesigns.co.uk

Published by Little Nell Publishing
At The Old Curiosity Bookshop, Hathern, Leicestershire. www.oldcuriositybookshop.co.uk
No part of this publication may be reproduced, stored in a retrieval system or transmitted in any form by any means, electronic, mechanical, photocopying, recording or otherwise, without the prior permission of the Author.
This book is sold subject to the condition that it shall not, by way of trade or otherwise, be lent, re-sold, hired out or otherwise circulated without the Author's prior consent in any form or cover other than that in which it is published and without a similar condition including this condition being imposed on the subsequent purchaser.

Typeset in Plantin Light

"You beat cancer by how you live, why you live and in the manner in which you live."

Stuart Scott

For Tom, thank you for listening...

and

All who have fought and lost, are fighting now and who have fought and won...

DISCLAIMER:

The information in this book is intended for general information only. It is not intended to amount to advice on which you should rely, and is not a substitute for diagnosis, treatment or advice from your doctor or any qualified and experienced health professional.

This book is compiled using a vast number of varied sources available to anyone on the subject of illness and cancer, its prevention and cure. Much of the information in this book is already in the public domain and can be accessed freely by any reader.

Whilst the author has made every effort to ensure that the facts, information and conclusions are accurate and as up to date as possible at the time of publication, the author and publisher assume no responsibility for errors, omissions or their consequences.

The author is not a Doctor of Medicine and so is not qualified to give any advice on medical matters. Cancer, as well as all other illnesses can be serious. Illness is an individual disease. Readers must consult with experts and specialists in the appropriate medical field before taking, or refraining from taking, any action.

The author intends this book to be an information source and not a source of any advice. The author and the publisher cannot be held responsible for any actions that are taken by any reader as a result of information contained in the text of this book. Such action is taken entirely at the reader's own risk.

Contents

Foreword by Steven Johns
Introduction by Paula Reed
Why I Wrote This Book
Chapter 1 My Story Part 1
    A Very Bad Start in Life
Chapter 2 My Story Part 2
    School Days
Chapter 3 My Story Part 3
    Off to Work I Go...

Chapter 4 My Story Part 4
        Flying High
Chapter 5   *Who Are You?*
Chapter 6   *The Search Begins*
Chapter 7
*Prevention **IS** Better Than Cure*
Chapter 8
Finding Yourself – Onion Therapy
Chapter 9 *The Power of Your Mind*
Chapter 10
What If I Already Have Cancer?
Chapter 11
What About the Carers?
Chapter 12 *Death is an Option*
Chapter 13   *Doctors Read This*
Chapter 14 Resources
      Information is Power
Afterword & Acknowledgements
Foreword and Introduction to Onion Therapy

by Steven Johns MA

Paula and I were about 8 months into the writing of this book when the final title popped out on one of our coaching sessions. The original title we'd come up with was Cancer Evasion and I'd had an idea for the front cover: I wanted to put Tax Evasion with the word Tax crossed out and substituted by CANCER in a bold red handwritten font. We were discussing - no, wrong word - *dissecting* beliefs, together with our thoughts and perspectives on them, when we both came to a simultaneous conclusion that the cause of many beliefs and predicaments in a person's life can be stripped down to a single start point.

In the case of cancer, if it were possible to go back to the very moment the first mutated cell divided and replicated its tumescent self, you would find the cause or causes of that individual's disease right there all around them. The environment they were in, the stresses they had to deal with, the trauma that was hurting them, the family genes they possessed, the abuse they were suffering from, all played their part at a certain moment in their life. By the time there are any symptoms it's usually considered to be developed so far that drastic toxic treatment or radical surgery seem to be the only options available. Also, by then much time has passed, often years, and the real cause is disguised, hidden and buried by a great many layers of life that have grown around it, like a callous around a splinter.

We ploughed on after our Eureka moment and soon, within a few minutes, we had developed this most elegant metaphor - Onion Therapy. Peel an onion, keep removing the layers, layer after layer and what do you have? Right there in the middle of an onion? Nothing!

In the case of a belief (which, by the way, is usually limiting the holder from moving on in their life) there's a single event, influence or experience which is nearly always hidden from the conscious mind and in itself is apparently unrelated to the later problem. Paula and I know this from our training in behavioural neuro therapies. (EFT in Paula's case and NLP in mine – see the resources section at the end of the book for more details.) Phobias, fears and aversions all stem from our past and often begin when we are children. The cures that release us from these burdens engage therapies which strip away the layers of false evidence and the misguided sub-conscious protection that is holding us back. Once the start point is exposed for what it is, the whole (holistic) mind understands, and progress is usually very swift thereafter; in the case of phobias it's most often instantaneous.

We then made the connection with cancer and the work and observation that Paula has done with the Loughborough Cancer Self-Help group, of which you'll read more throughout the book. We discussed the tantalising possibility that in many cases it could be belief that is driving and accelerating the progress of many diseases. How many times have we heard of the friend who has been diagnosed with a cancer which the consultant oncologist has labelled as TERMINAL? Our friend, and everyone around them, believes that to be and thus their death sentence begins. But what happens when you turn that belief on its head?

We have all heard of a miracle happening, and Paula has seen cancer sufferers who have recovered after all other conventional hope is lost. In all these cases, a positive belief in being able to overcome the illness and to live on was powerfully present.

Once we had got this far, we started to look at many aspects of life and how a positive change can be effected by going back to a core point and then moving on from there. We looked at diets, fitness, health and well-being, careers, relationships, nutrition and all manner of worthy subjects many of us struggle to get right, maintain and to fully understand…

Paula Reed BSc (Hons) MBPsS is a holistic and complimentary therapist who runs her own practice from her home in Barrow Upon Soar, Leicestershire. For ten years now she has helped to run The Loughborough Cancer Self-help Group and has discovered how alternative treatments and therapies can offer help and hope often after conventional medicine has failed. She also knows that the very best way to evade cancer is through living a healthy and positively mindful life. She knows too, that is also the very best way to live life even without the threat of cancer.

I have read many books and studied a good deal about what makes people become better at whatever sport, profession, discipline, technique and so on that took my fancy at a time in my life when I had the time. They have often been written by some worthy author of note who grew up in a land of plenty with the benefit of a loving family and paid-for education and training that didn't involve having to work for a living too early in the third decade of their time on this planet. This is not so for Paula Reed. I'd say that all she has learned has been learned on a very hard road and you need to read her story first to see how she has come to know what she wants you all to know.

So, in the true spirit of Onion Therapy, we'll get back to the very core, the essence and the start point of what may well be the most valuable and life-enhancing book you have ever read.

*   *   *

Introduction by Paula Reed

Why did I write this book?

The first answer is for me.

I have always held the belief that I am "not good enough" and I am by no means unique. Many people I know have the same belief. What many of us don't know, is that beliefs are buried so deep in the subconscious mind they can affect everything we do. The way we think is consciously and subconsciously governed by our beliefs and it can be difficult to change them - but it can be done, and I will show you how. My belief of "not being good enough" held me back and stopped me from reaching my full potential – until I started on this book that is. It is proof to me that "I am good enough" but I'll let you be the judge of that.

The second answer is that I am writing it for you. Cancer Evasion was the first title we gave it, as you will have read in Steve's introduction, and in that regard it does exactly what it says on the tin, almost. If it were that easy all you would have to do is to read this book to avoid getting cancer in the first place. I want to share with you all the information I have amassed over 30 years of research on health and wellbeing in general and the information I have gained over the last 10 years by researching, working with, and observing people with cancer. Cancer is both preventable and curable – but more about this later.

The statistics produced by Cancer Research UK in 2015 are both shocking and frightening. They show that 1 in 2 people born in the UK after 1960 will be diagnosed with some form of cancer in their lifetime and that a person's risk of developing it depends on many factors: including age, genetics, lifestyle and exposure to risk factors. Around 4 in 10 UK cancer cases every year could be prevented. That's more than 135,000 every year. And it won't surprise you to know that smoking is the largest cause of cancer in the UK.

There is nothing we can do about our genetics, but they only contribute 5% to the risk and, according to Bruce Lipton, a renowned cellular biologist, it is only 1%. The other 95+%, apart from age, is something we can definitely do something about. Just changing our diet, exercising more, removing stress and avoiding toxins is a highly effective way of building up the body's immune system. A healthy immune system results in a healthy body, a body in which cancer struggles to survive. All the information is out there but it takes mountains of time and effort to find it. The good news is that I have done it for you in this book.

Understanding what you need to do is one thing but doing it is another and that requires a different mind-set; that's where Steve and I worked together to develop Onion Therapy which, as you will now know, is the title I finally decided upon.

I also look at the big question of why people who do all of those things still get cancer or why some people are cured and then after a while it comes back. Is it possible that mainstream medicine fails to look for "what caused the cancer in the first place"?   If you sustain an injury and you go to the doctors, the first thing you will be asked is how you did it, because if the doctor knows the cause he will have a better idea of how to treat it effectively. And yet, when a cancer is diagnosed seldom does one ask about, or try to ascertain, the cause. Additionally, people diagnosed with cancer are usually treated in the same way, despite the fact that everyone's cancer is unique. These two factors should not be ignored if you want the best outcome.   You might get rid of the symptoms but if you don't get rid of the cause it will keep coming back.

You may, at this point, be wondering how it is possible to ascertain the cause of any individual's cancer. No one can ever really be certain but there are clues in the life experiences and the traumas they have gone through, both physical and emotional and the beliefs they have formed as a result.   Beliefs again! They're so powerful and will be popping up everywhere in this book.   It's because they lie deep in the subconscious mind, that part of the mind that operates automatically in order to keep you a breathing, digesting, seeing, hearing, tasting, safe, functioning human being.   These beliefs are usually formed very early on, and we hang on to them for our dear lives, but they can be changed - something I will be covering in more detail later on.

So, according to the statistics, a high percentage of you reading this book will have, or have had, cancer; reading this book will teach you how to harness your body's own healing power so that it has the potential of reversing it, managing it or healing it.   Alas, not everyone is going to be healed because the oft bandied phrase 'All cancer is curable, but all people are not' resounds loud and clear here.   Why is that?   What is it that makes the difference?   Although I don't have all the answers, I have information, tips and techniques that I want to share with you, that *could* make the difference.

When I first started writing Onion Therapy, I intended it to be simply a compilation of resources, a self - help book for people with cancer and for those who want to avoid getting cancer in the first place. But as is so often the story with plans, that is not how it turned out. As I started to write, something very strange happened, I found I was writing about me and everything that had happened to me in my life. Once I started writing I couldn't stop, it just kept flowing, so much so, that many times I had to stop because my arm ached from writing so much. Whilst I found writing it all down to be both emotional and cathartic, it also made me realise how much living in a continual state of stress through most of my life had affected my physical, mental and emotional health. Even doctors agree that 90% of physical issues are caused by stress of some kind.

This realisation led me to re-plan the book and to include my lifelong quest to resolve my own issues and the things I had to go through to get to where I am today; how I dealt with my stress and how I learned how to change my beliefs and mindset.
So, the first part of this book is about me, it is my story.

Thereafter it contains over 30 years of my research compiled in one place. It has information that you may not have come across before. Information based on alternative therapies which are many and various, and which can be used in two ways. They can be used as an alternative to traditional medicine, or they can be used to complement it. Most people use a combination of both, however for those who have been told that there is nothing more traditional medicine can offer, alternative therapies are their only hope.

Information is power; it enables you to take control of your health and make informed choices based on the full picture and not just a fragment of it. Our genetic makeup, our DNA, and our life experience make us unique, which means we all make different choices. Choices that resonate with what makes sense to us, choices we believe in. When things are not working and we are not getting well, information enables us to make changes because "if you keep on doing what you always do, you will keep on getting what you always get". Making changes based on all the information available could make the difference as to whether we get well or not. This book will provide you with a big chunk of all that's out there and the more information you have the more power you have.

There are hundreds of self-help books out there, but this book is different. In addition to providing information about alternative therapies, you will learn about the most important component of health – the power of the mind. Not only can it make the difference as to whether you get a disease or overcome disease, it can also make the difference as to whether you achieve or not. If used properly this component can be applied to anything and everything in life to create a positive outcome. The very fact that I am writing this book is proof, as until I learned how to change my belief of "not being good enough" I was held back and was being prevented from making my dream a reality.

My personal journey to get to where I am today, what I had to go through to get here, together with being under constant stress had a seriously negative effect on my health. But that is not the whole story. Like me you are likely to be shackled, bound by your own beliefs, 70% of which are negative. Not only is your health being affected but many other aspects of your life are held back from progress. In my personal journey you will read about how I deal with my stress and how I have learnt to utilise the power of my mind to change my beliefs; and in this book you will learn how you can change those beliefs that are stopping you from moving forward.

The power of beliefs cannot be underestimated. It doesn't matter how healthily you eat, how much exercise you do, how well you are dealing with stress or how positive you are, you will still be a perfect target for cancer. Unless you know how to engage all of your senses and learn how to change your beliefs to feel positive, you are likely to fail to achieve your goals. If you can tap into the power of your mind that can change. I am a natural sceptic but over the years I have seen and read about so many people who have healed themselves of cancer and people who have managed their cancer to outlive their given prognosis, that my beliefs have changed. These survivors had one thing in common - they believed in the possibility that they could get better, which gave them hope. I know it was a deep-down subconscious belief that was the catalyst to their survival. There is evidence all around demonstrating the power of beliefs: In cultures where voodoo is practised, perfectly healthy young individuals die after a curse has been put on them, placebos work if people believe they are taking a medicine that helps, and not if they don't. In a recent study on depression 81% of people given the placebo responded as if they had been given the drug. We have all been brought up to believe that when we are ill, we go to the doctors, and he or she will take care of it; we have learned that the responsibility of taking care of our health can be offloaded to another.   In handing healthcare over to our doctor, we have effectively given away our control, the control to use our innate ability to heal ourselves.   Worse still, not only do people give away control to their doctor but they mostly believe what they are told. So, when a doctor tells a patient they have only got six months to live, whether it is true or not he has instilled in them a belief that is, in effect, a death sentence, and I have witnessed this so many times.

So, the adage 'your life is in their hands' is made true, but I show you on these pages how to change that, how to take back control and put your life in *your* hands.
This is truly empowering.

Onion Therapy considers all four aspects of health: the physical, mental, emotional and spiritual.
   Onion Therapy is a comprehensive book of information on alternative therapies, with a list of books and links to resources and more information.

   Onion Therapy is my story, my personal journey and what I went through to improve my health and my life.

Onion Therapy is about the power of the mind and how stress and beliefs, both positive and negative, can have an impact on every aspect of our lives.

In conclusion Onion Therapy not only provides information on what you need to do to enjoy better health, but it teaches you how to do it and it maintains that, if you make these changes, not only will you enjoy better health, but you will experience a better life too - I promise you.

*   *   *

Then mother left us, and the angle of the candlelight grew narrower on the wall, and finally went out, closing that day forever.

Laurie Lee – Village Christmas

Chapter 1
MY STORY
Part 1

A Very Bad Start in Life

Given the choice my Mum wouldn't have had children at all, but she was from a devout Roman Catholic family, and it was her solemn duty. She was thirty-three when I was born in the Leicester Royal Infirmary sixty-one years ago and I was her firstborn. She'd had a very difficult pregnancy and to top that she developed what we now know as severe post-natal depression and all but rejected me. Every opportunity she had she would palm me off onto anyone and everyone for as long as she could. Not the best start in life. I don't know whether it was because she never really recovered from her depression, but she always made it clear that having me had ruined her life and often told me in frustration and anger that she could not tolerate me at any price. As a result, my early years were very difficult. I tried in every way possible to get her attention, but no matter what I did, it never worked.

When I was nine months old my Mum became pregnant again and my sister Carole was born. Carole was a very sickly and weak baby as she had been born with a ruptured diaphragm and couldn't keep her feed down. She had to have an operation to correct it and then was in a plaster cast chair for many months. Ironically, Mum took to Carole even though she was much more demanding than I had ever been this meant I was side-lined still further, creating ever more emotional distance between me and my Mum. I've learned all this from family and friends as I grew older.

My Dad was the gardener at Ratcliffe College, a private Catholic boarding school near Sileby, Leicestershire, and we lived in an idyllic setting in a tied house in the grounds of the college. But as a little girl, with no-one to play with and a mother who didn't want me, I felt lonely, isolated, abandoned and far removed from the lucky recipient of idyllic surroundings.

Well, not quite. There was a lady I called Auntie Evelyn who lived with her husband Jack in one of the other houses about five minutes away from us in the school grounds.   Jack had worked at the school for many years and had recently retired; he suffered from ill health and had very limited mobility.   Auntie Evelyn loved him dearly and spent all her time looking after him. Both Jack and Evelyn loved children but had never been able to have any of their own.   They were delighted when we came along, and Mum took us to see them.   Auntie Evelyn would visit us too, but Uncle Jack was unable, so she had to come on her own.   This was an excellent arrangement all round as it gave Mum a break and meant that I got the attention I so badly craved.

Once Carole got well and grew older, I had someone to play with.   I loved her dearly, and still do, although we both have very different personalities.   I took after my Mum, apparently, and was hyperactive, on the go all the time, questioned everything and had a fiery disposition. Carole on the other hand took after my Dad, very mild mannered, cool, calm and totally laid back. The relationship between Mum and me never improved and it was made worse because having really taken to Carole, she made her the favourite. This must have had an effect on me because (as I have been told in later life) I tried to set fire to Carole's pram when I was three.

When I was four, we moved from the house in the school grounds to a small semi-detached house in Sileby which belonged to the school.   I remember feeling happy and sad all at the same time - I would no longer be near Auntie Evelyn and Uncle Jack but I had the enticing prospect of new friends to play with. Shortly after moving it was time for me to start school.

Devout Catholics insist on their children attending a Catholic school. The nearest one for me was in Loughborough. This meant a twenty-minute walk to the bus stop, followed by a half hour bus ride and then a ten minute walk the other end. A frightful ordeal for little me, but Mum did accompany me in that first week. I was terrified and clung on to her for dear life, until she managed to free herself from me.   I had never been to playschool or nursery, which were almost unheard of in those days, and so for me and most children this was the first time we had been separated by any distance from our parents. It was a big shock to the system, I cried and cried and cried. I was inconsolable, but in the end the teacher sat me on a table with some older children who were playing, and it wasn't long before I became involved. For a short while I was able to distract myself from this all-consuming feeling of fear, but I was relieved to see Mum at the end of the school day. I guess the separation trauma I experienced is the same for most first-born children, for it is they who pave the way for their siblings. After several days I was beginning to get used to the whole process, although I can't honestly say that I liked it.   After a week Mum stopped coming on the bus with me and put me in the care of Karen, a ten-year-old girl who went to my school and was used to travelling on her own.   Karen appeared nice at first, but I was slow and lagged behind which annoyed her; she shouted at me, hit me and threatened me with all sorts of things.   I never told anyone about it even though it continued for months until I was familiar with the route and knew the times of the buses and then I could do it by myself. Because Mum still thought Karen was looking after me, she left me to my own devices. I neither liked nor disliked school but I did make a lot of friends and for some reason became popular with my peers.   I was also a model pupil, obeyed all the rules, and didn't give the teachers any problems, so they liked me too, which was something I had never really been used to at home.

I was eight years old when Mum was diagnosed with lung cancer.   Mum and Dad both smoked - people did in those days. It wasn't long after the diagnosis that Mum was admitted to hospital to have most of one lung removed.   She was in hospital for several weeks before being allowed home to recover. It was the school summer holiday and, while Dad was at work, I had to stay in to look after her.   I was angry and resentful; it was lovely and sunny, and I wanted to go out to play with my friends.   Carole was allowed out to play, but not me; I had to stay in and look after Mum. She had a walking stick by her bed and when she wanted something, she'd bang on the floor with it.   I'd go upstairs, she would tell me what she wanted and then I'd either do it or fetch it.   When I had completed the task, I was allowed to go back downstairs. On one occasion when I forgot to shut the door, she became hysterical, very aggressive and shouted at me. Not wanting to upset her again, I made sure when I left the next time that I shut the door - only to be shouted at again and told to leave the door open.   No matter what I did I could not do anything right. What I didn't know was that Mum had an infection which was making her delirious and behave in a totally irrational way. After a few days Dad called the doctor who sent her to hospital straight away and that was the last time I ever saw her.

She was in hospital for several weeks before she died, and Dad thought it best to prepare us so that it wasn't such a shock; he told Carole and me that Mum was not going to get better. We kept asking to see her, but Dad had made the decision that it was not in Mum's best interest or ours for us to visit her in hospital, as she was very ill and heavily drugged. He thought it would upset us to see her looking so ill. He wanted us to remember Mum as she was when she was fit and well, not how she was when she was poorly. Although he thought he was doing the right thing, he wasn't. Every day when I came home from school I slowed down as I approached the house, wondering if I was going to be told she had died. Just waiting for the inevitable, and not knowing when it would be, was awful. As the weeks went by, I used to wish that she would die; the stress, night after night, was becoming unbearable. Then when she did die, I felt guilty for wishing her dead. Dad was also wrong in not telling Carole and me when Mum's funeral was, and not allowing us to go. But things were very different when we were young, and it was rare that children went to a funeral.

When I began to write my story, I had no intention of giving an account of the sexual abuse I experienced, which started shortly after my Mum died. However, difficult as it is, I feel I need to fill in more detail to help those of you who may have experienced the same and, like me, have never been able to speak about it. One of the reasons I didn't speak about it was that I felt guilty and ashamed; I thought it was my fault and I didn't want to admit to myself or anyone else that I was complicit in such horrible things. The other reason, I now know, lies much deeper. Because it was so traumatic, the whole experience was buried deep in my subconscious mind. As a result, I spent many years trying to squash it down using food as my coping mechanism. Other abused people that I have spoken to tell me that they can relate to that; some use food, others alcohol and/or drugs to make them feel better and to stop the painful emotions from surfacing. But whilst ever these emotions are buried, they will be constantly playing in the background, draining your energy, and having a detrimental effect on your life. That is why it is so important to seek help early on - sooner or later it will raise its ugly head. The time will come when you will no longer be able to cope with it and you will be forced to deal with it just as I had to. I can look back on it now and think how awful it was, how sad it was, but the mixed emotions I used to feel whenever I thought about it are no longer there. I can write about it factually and I don't feel anything, it is just as if I am talking about someone else. I can never change what happened, but I was able to change the way I feel about what happened and you can do the same. I hope that sharing my personal journey of how I got to this stage will inspire you to share your troubles and traumas, as this is proof that I not only survived but I thrived as a result.

So, I need to tell you about Michael. He worked as a gardener with my Dad at the College. He had previously been in care, but when he was sixteen the authorities abandoned him; he had to leave the care home and had been sleeping rough for quite some time. In those days there was very little support for people like Michael and so Ratcliffe College were asked if they could take him in and give him a job. Michael was very much a loner, not very well educated and had no support or contact from his family but he was a hard worker. Dad really liked him and treated him like a son. Initially he lived at Ratcliffe College and slept in a dormitory. He had all his meals at the college, and they did all his washing too. This was okay but it wasn't ideal, so Dad put forward an idea. There was an old potting shed in the grounds (just around the corner from where Auntie Evelyn lived) which could easily and cheaply be converted into a small bedsit. It just needed a partitioning wall to separate the bedroom from the main room, a sink putting in and some electrical points. It didn't need to have a toilet as there was one outside and Michael could have a shower or bath at the College. The College liked the idea and soon Michael had his own space. They kitted him out with a single metal dormitory bed together with bedlinen, rugs and a few items of furniture. They continued to do his washing and he was still able to have all his meals in college too. It was an ideal arrangement for all parties. Dad trusted Michael one hundred percent and my sister, and I often visited him when we were being looked after by Auntie Evelyn. Sometimes we would go together and sometimes on our own. I liked to go to watch television and to listen to his collection of records, as it was an escape for me. There was another reason I liked to go there too - he smoked.

After Mum died, I lost most of the parental control which I knew. Dad was out at work when we got home from school and, on many evenings, he would be at the pub, so I tried all sorts of things that kids weren't supposed to try, and one of them was smoking. I'd search the ashtrays at home for nub ends and sometimes steal a cigarette or two out of Dad's packet he'd left on the kitchen table. So, one day I asked Michael if I could have a cigarette. Initially he didn't want to give me one as he said I wasn't old enough and Dad wouldn't like it. Not one to take no for an answer I kept working on him until eventually he gave in. The problem was the more cigarettes I smoked the more I craved; I felt they helped me to relax, and they numbed my mind.

I can't remember exactly when it first happened, but I can remember vividly what happened. I must have been around nine or ten as I had just lost my Mum; I was emotionally raw and very vulnerable. I can remember sitting on the bed in Michael's bedsit watching television with him sitting next to me. I was in my school uniform: white blouse, striped tie, navy skirt and beige knee-high socks. I had kicked off my brown lace-up shoes before sitting on the bed. All of a sudden, I felt his hand on my right knee. I thought this was strange, so I pushed his hand away and asked him what he was doing. "Nothing," he said. Then a few minutes later it happened again, this time his hand was above my knee and under my skirt. I felt uncomfortable and irritated; once again I pushed his hand away and asked him what he was doing. Same reply, "Nothing". I just couldn't understand what was going on as this had never happened before, and I didn't like it. This continued and each time his hand went further and further up my leg until eventually he put his fingers inside my knickers. I was stunned, shocked and felt awful as I knew this was wrong. I told him to stop it and that I didn't like it, but he continued regardless. He told me I was very beautiful, that he was attracted to me, and he was going to show me what it was like to be grown up. If I trusted him and let him do what he wanted to do I would like it; it would be pleasurable, and I would feel good. I had never heard anything like this before. On the one hand I was flattered yet on the other I knew I didn't like it and it felt wrong, but he had caught me at a very vulnerable time. Having lost my Mum, I was feeling abandoned and unloved - and I thought there was something wrong with me. So, for a split second I decided to go with it as anything that would make me feel good was worth a try. As I stopped resisting, he began to move his fingers further into my knickers and I began to tingle all over. It did feel nice although I didn't want it to; this was very wrong, and I knew I shouldn't be doing it. I was so confused but the pleasant feeling masked all the other stresses in my life. After a while he stopped and then he offered me a cigarette – without me having to ask for one. He was treating me like an equal, a grown up, I felt special and really thought I was getting the attention I craved. I thoroughly enjoyed that cigarette as it helped to numb me even more, but I still didn't feel right and felt sick in my stomach.

Afterwards I couldn't stop thinking about what had happened and what I had done. I felt mixed emotions: excitement, guilt, shame, all rolled into one. I couldn't tell anybody and so I had to keep it bottled up inside. I suppose I was on the brink of physically becoming a woman but still had the mind of a child. With all that was already churning away in my little brain this was another stressful confusion to deal with when I had so many.

Deep down I knew I shouldn't go back there again but I did, many times. It made me feel special. Each visit he would put pressure on me to let him do more things. Not physical pressure but emotional pressure and, if I refused, he would bribe me with cigarettes. Anyone with an addiction will know that you will do anything to get a fix and that's just what I did. And so, as time went on, I found myself masturbating him until he ejaculated, at the same time allowing him to masturbate me. Fortunately, it didn't usually take too long, but even so it seemed like an age, and I couldn't wait for it to be over so I could have another cigarette. The worst thing he made me do was to let him put his penis in my mouth. It tasted vile and he pushed it so hard and deep into my mouth I felt I was choking. He made me suck it while he masturbated himself and then, when he ejaculated, he made me swallow the semen. I will never forget the horrible, salty, warm taste - thinking about it now makes me feel sick. What on earth was I doing to myself? All for attention and a few cigarettes? Sometimes I would cry afterwards because I felt so desperate and couldn't see a way out. I don't know how long it went on for, but it must have been about three years, until I met Jeremy, my first boyfriend.

It was then that I managed to pluck up the courage to tell Michael that I didn't want to do it anymore and much to my surprise he didn't seem to mind. Strange as it may seem, this hurt me. I thought I had been really special to him and assumed he would be upset. Obviously, he wasn't, and I now know why - he was abusing my sister as well.

During the time I was being abused by Michael, I also began to be abused by the son of one of Dad's friends. One day he came to see Dad, but Dad was at the pub as usual, so he decided to stay and talk to me. He told me he was attracted to me and, as he started to touch me, I went cold and froze on the spot. "Oh my God! Why does this keep happening? It must be me; something must be wrong with me."

All he wanted to do was to touch me while he masturbated himself. As he was a smoker, I thought I could use this to my advantage, so I told him that was okay, but I wanted some cigarettes in return. He agreed and so this arrangement continued until I met Jeremy and told him I wasn't going to do it anymore. He didn't give up as easily as Michael and tried to persuade me to carry on, but I stood my ground. Eventually he got the message and left me alone. So, for a while, I was free from all the stress; but I was a teenager in love and that comes with other stresses, as I was later to find out.

However, that was not the end of my abuse. One night one of my Dad's drunken friends tried to get into my bed while I was asleep. I woke up in terror as he was trying to force himself on me. My sister heard the commotion, came into my bedroom and dragged him off of me. He resisted but after a long hard fight we got him off and shouted so loud that he ran downstairs and out into the street. I can't remember where Dad was, probably at the pub and the door must have been unlocked. I was so upset, not just for me, but for my sister too. She was much younger and shouldn't have to deal with things like that.

Once again this reinforced my feeling of not being good enough, that something was wrong with me, and I blamed myself. I just didn't know what to do. And still it continued. One day my best friend's dad saw me walking home and stopped to offer me a lift. I got in the car, and we were talking when suddenly, in a remote area, he pulled into the side of the road and stopped the engine. I felt tense, uncomfortable and I had a gut feeling that something was going to happen. My gut instinct was right. He turned towards me and told me he thought I was very pretty, and did I know I had lovely big brown eyes. I was terrified. I couldn't believe this was happening. My Dad's drunken friends were one thing, but this was my best friend's dad! Someone I liked because I thought he was a real family man, kind and caring. Someone I respected and looked up to yet, here he was, going to take advantage of me. This was surreal. I froze and prayed to God to help me and thankfully he did. Suddenly my friend's dad must have realised that this was not a good idea, so he started the engine and drove me home acting as if nothing had happened. Well, you could argue that nothing did but only because he thought better of it. I was so relieved to get out of that car, I felt angry, numb, sick and sorry for myself all over again. I couldn't understand why this kept happening to me. What he did had a big impact on my life then, because I didn't want to visit my friend anymore and couldn't tell her why. She thought I had fallen out with her. I couldn't face seeing her dad as things could never be the same again and I didn't want to see her mum because I felt somehow it was my fault and couldn't help thinking of the consequences if anyone ever found out.

Well now they have because I am telling you.
Why am I telling you? Because both my sister and I were so affected by these events that for years we had trouble forming relationships. We found the physical side very hard, not pleasurable, which meant we avoided sex at all costs. When we did have sex, we had flashbacks and although we were with someone who was loving and caring, the feelings were the same as if we were being abused all over again.

I think it's important to tell you what happened to Michael. When my sister's first husband died, she was so traumatized that she went for counselling. One of the things that came out of it was that she was so full of anger at how the abuse had affected her life, she decided to report it to the police. It was only when she asked me if I had been abused that I found out about her abuse. When she told me about her experience I was horrified, as it was far worse than mine. I was nine but she was only seven, trying to come to terms with losing Mum and being abused as well. Not only that, but she also told me that she was being bullied at school too. I was so sad as I'd had no idea. When she asked me if I would support her by giving a statement to the police, I had mixed feelings. Of course, I would support her, but this was going to bring up all the things that I didn't want to think about and, believe it or not, I felt sorry for Michael as he had been abused as a child, was rejected by his family and didn't have any friends.

Making a statement to the young male police officer was one of the hardest things I have ever done. Not only was it embarrassing, but it brought up all those feelings of guilt and shame and that I blamed myself, because I felt complicit in what happened. Young and green as he was, the police officer said something that stopped me in my tracks.

"You were only a child, and it was not your fault."

At that moment I knew he was right. I had been "only a child", a vulnerable child, and Michael took away my innocence. I had been groomed and I was well under the age of being able to consent to any of it.

Carole and I made our statements and expected to hear something, but nothing happened. Nothing happened until nine years later when Carole needed more counselling as she had been struggling with depression. Again, the anger she felt about her abuse came up and she re - contacted the police to see what had happened to Michael. It then became clear that due to a series of administrative errors the paperwork had been mislaid and the case had been forgotten. The police apologised profusely, and the case was immediately resurrected with my sister and I having to go through the trauma of making another statement. It was horrendous, but this time Michael was arrested straight away, his flat was searched, and his computer confiscated. When the police examined his computer, they found that he had been viewing images of child pornography, and when he was charged Michael pleaded guilty. He also pleaded guilty to abusing me and Carole. The fact that he pleaded guilty meant we were not required to go to court to give evidence and I can't tell you how relieved we were not to have to be interrogated in front of a court room full of people. But Carole wanted to go to court to see him convicted and I went with her. When I saw Michael in the dock, I hardly recognised him. He was in his sixties, had very little hair and looked old and frail. He was handcuffed to a police officer and his head was lowered. I felt very sad. I don't remember much about the rest of the proceedings until the judge announced the sentence of 9 years. My sister was so happy, it was as if a big weight had been lifted off her, at last she felt justice had been done. On the other hand, I felt quite numb and sorry for Michael. I forgave him and hoped that he would be able to cope with prison and all that that entailed. I knew there was a code within the criminal fraternity and that child abusers were looked on as the worst kind of offenders, suffering all kinds of abuse as a result. You might think he got what he deserved and how could I possibly forgive him? My answer is this: I didn't forgive his behaviour, that is unforgiveable, but I did forgive him and the two are very different. By doing this I was able to let it go and move on.

It took a lot of courage for me to write this as not only am I exposing myself but also my sister and our perpetrator, who at the time of writing is still in prison. When I spoke to my sister about it, she was in full agreement that I should write this in order to help others. If there is one message that I want to give to those of you who have suffered abuse as a child and who believe it is your fault it is this: remember what the police officer said to me, "You were only a child, and it was not your fault."

Do not let the abuse you suffered make you a victim. Do not let it ruin your life. Do something about it sooner rather than later before it takes a hold on you. In this book you will find plenty of information and different ways of disconnecting from the emotions you feel. Do your research and find the one that is right for you but do it now. You can never change the situation, but you can change the way you feel about it, just as I did, and that will change your life.

*   *   *

Chapter 2
MY STORY
Part Two

School days

Back in the mid-1960s it was unusual for a man to take responsibility for looking after his children, as it was always considered a woman's job, but that's what my Dad had to do. It was not easy, and he had to fight hard to keep us. He had to convince the authorities that he was fit to do it and that he could be there for us when we went to school and came home. The college management were very understanding and supportive, they allowed him to work around school times and so it was agreed he could keep us. But Carole and I knew how fragile this situation was and we lived in constant fear that we would be taken into care. Dad had always had a drink problem, but he'd managed to keep it under control until the trauma of Mum's death. Afterwards it was very hard for him to hold down a job as well as care for us, so he began drinking more and more, soon becoming alcohol dependent until eventually he became an alcoholic.

He went to the pub most nights and left us on our own at home; he told us we must not let anyone know or we would be taken away from him. I worried that our neighbours would question us about Dad and his whereabouts, and I knew that I couldn't let them know that we were being left alone and that Dad was drinking, so I developed the ability to lie convincingly. Whenever anyone asked where Dad was, I would say he was not well and was in bed or anything that came to mind that was logical. I felt miserable inside about telling lies but we couldn't let anyone know he was leaving us home alone or Dad would not be allowed to bring us up.

There was one incident in particular which involved my next-door neighbour: She was always watching us and would wait at the front gate for us to come home from school. At weekends she'd watch us from behind her net curtains. She would question me at every opportunity, every time I ventured outside; she pretended to be kind and caring but I knew she was just trying to catch me out. I avoided her whenever possible, returning home via the back road where our garages were and entering the house through the back door so she wouldn't see me. Coming and going out of the back door was not always practical or possible, so when I had to come out of the front door, I would try to sneak out quickly when she was not looking and run like hell down the road. However, there were two slab steps at the front door which clunked every time they were stepped on, usually alerting my nosey neighbour, and on this particular day she caught me. After a bit of smarmy small talk from her to lull me into a false sense of security there came the usual question, "Is your Dad in?" I told her he was, but he was having a nap.
"Do you think you could ask him to pop round when he has a minute? It's not urgent," she said, "when he wakes up will be fine."

I remember feeling trapped because I was going to get caught out lying. I would have to go to the pub and tell Dad to come home. I went back into the house and told Carole what had happened so the two of us snuck out of the back door and ran all the way to the pub. Children were not allowed in pubs, so we had to open the door to the bar and try to get Dad's attention without the landlord seeing us. Eventually he came out and I told him about the neighbour wanting to see him; I begged him to come home, or she would report us, and we would be taken away. He told me not to be so silly, he wasn't bothered about her and told us to go home. Terrified, I begged him, "Please, Dad, please!" I must have sounded so desperate and frightened that he agreed to come home after he had finished his pint. Eventually he appeared and the three of us started to make our way back home. Dad was drunk and couldn't walk straight, swaying from side to side. Carole and I took an arm each trying to steady him so that he wouldn't fall over or stagger into the road. My Dad was a big man, and it was hard work. I wondered how he ever got home every night in that state. When we were nearly home, I told him we should go up the back road in case we were seen. He wasn't happy about that as it was muddy and full of potholes but after much pleading, we got in by the back door.

Once he had got himself together, he went around to the neighbour. He seemed to be gone for ages and eventually returned smiling, assuring us that everything was okay. But the constant worry about being taken into care never went away until my sixteenth birthday when I knew I was safe.

Pretending things were 'normal' meant that I was always under stress, constantly living in fear and on high alert all the time. I was only a child, but I could not be like other children as I had to take responsibility not only for myself and Carole but my Dad too; I became like a parent to him because he didn't manage at all well. I worried about his health; I worried when he was drunk and late coming home from the pub - I worried that something had happened to him - that he had fallen or been hit by a car because he often ended up staggering into the road. I also worried that he would die in his sleep, and I would spend the night listening to his breathing and snoring; if I couldn't hear anything, I would get out of bed to go and check he was okay.

It had always been my Mum's dream that my sister and I would be educated at the local Convent School as it had an excellent reputation. The Convent was a private Catholic school and pupils had to pay fees to attend. However, if you were a Catholic who couldn't afford to pay and you passed the 11+ exam you were eligible to take the Convent entrance exam - the school allocated two free places to the top pupils, six assisted places where you paid half fees and the rest had to pass the exam in order to get a place and pay full fees. Because I knew that it had been my mother's wish that I went to the Convent I made up my mind to work really hard to pass the 11+ exam, so that I could take the entrance exam and get a free place. Many of my school reports said I was 'average', and I usually came very near to the bottom of the class when it came to exams.

But I really worked my socks off to do well in this exam. I had to get a free place as my father, even with the help of my aunts, could never have afforded to pay. Much to everyone's amazement my hard work paid off - I came top and secured a free place. I was so pleased but one of my 'friends' soon put a damper on that. She had expected to get a free place, being always top or nearly top of the class while I was always nearly bottom. She told me that she should have had a free place and not me, and that I had only succeeded because the nuns felt sorry for me because my Mum had died. I was devastated; now I would never know if I had really done enough to pass. Not only had I lost what I'd considered a good friend, but I could not come to terms with how cruel and nasty she was and how much she had hurt me. It is only in later life that I realise how much of an impact this had on me and how it reinforced the belief that I wasn't good enough - a belief that started when I was rejected by my Mum. From then on achievement was always double edged, always believing that achievement was painful as well as pleasurable.

Transition from primary to secondary school is stressful enough for any child but the Convent expected much more from its pupils than most comprehensive schools; they were very strict disciplinarians, and the nuns didn't tolerate any bad behaviour or laziness while they pushed everyone to achieve very high standards. What should have been a pleasurable and fulfilling experience became a very difficult period especially with everything else that was going on in my life. I was now attending a 'posh school' where most of the pupils came from well off families for whom money was no object. I was the poor girl who didn't fit in and as if to emphasise this, Dad couldn't afford to buy me a new uniform, so I had to make do with a second hand one. Feeling I had nothing in common with most of the others, the survival mechanism I had developed by lying came to the fore again, which helped me to fit in and in my dream world I was one of them.

For example: During my early days at the Convent, I made friends with a lovely girl called Dominica. She was a boarder and from Monday to Friday she stayed in the school dormitory with other boarders. On Friday afternoons her brother would collect her to take her home for the weekend then bring her back on Sunday afternoons after tea. Although she had both a mum and a dad, her parents didn't really want her as they were too busy doing other things. Her dad ran a successful animal feed company and I think her mother spent a lot of time on committees, lunching, socializing and running the local WI. They were so busy that even when Dominica was at home she was left to her own devices. Despite the fact she appeared to have everything - a big house with acres of land, a beautifully decorated bedroom, lots of food, plenty of sweets and money, she didn't have what she really wanted and needed - her parents love and attention. I didn't know it at the time, but she felt unwanted and was very unhappy and lonely at school. She was on her own, very much like me; but in some ways, it was even worse for her knowing that she had parents who didn't want her, whereas my Mum was dead, and my Dad definitely wanted me and my sister - he just had a problem with alcohol. Dominica was very down to earth, never bragged about what she had, where she lived or the privileged lifestyle that was hers. Nevertheless, I knew our worlds were miles apart. So, when we talked about our lives, where we lived and what we had, I knew I just couldn't compete. She had central heating and her house was always warm, whereas I had a coal fire, and our house was always freezing, we even had ice on the inside of our windows. She had a state-of-the-art colour TV whereas Dad had rented a black and white one, but because he hadn't paid the rent on time the man in the shop came and took it away, so all we were left with was an old radio that didn't work very well. Dominica's mum employed a housekeeper who cooked, cleaned, ironed and looked after Dominica when her parents were out, which was most of the time. Her house was decorated, furnished and carpeted to a very high standard, whereas ours was badly in need of repair and decoration; our carpets were old and threadbare, and the furniture was not only wearing out, but it was old fashioned too. Her house was in the countryside, large and detached with six bedrooms and many acres of land – in stark contrast to our humble three bed semi-detached with an overgrown garden situated next door to factories.

In order to be more like Dominica I decided to let her think that I lived in a nice house and so I described my friend Karen's house who lived down the road (not the nasty Karen who used to take me to school). Her father was a factory manager, and her mum did work at home for the factory. The work was delivered on a Monday and collected on a Friday. This meant she was always at home for Karen and was able to cook lovely meals. They had enough money to decorate, furnish and carpet the house throughout with new modern things including a TV, and Karen's bedroom was beautiful although small. They had a Park Ray fire that heated radiators and the house was always warm. They also had a constant supply of hot water, so they could have a bath any time. We had to put the immersion heater on at least an hour before we wanted a bath and we had to be careful as it used a lot of electricity. My sister and I only had a bath once a week and we had to have one together in order to save water and electricity. The rest of the time we had to boil a kettle so that we could have a strip wash in front of the fire.

And so, when I was talking about my house to Dominica, and anyone else for that matter, Karen's house became my house. It was easy as I knew the house inside out and could never be caught out. Or could I? Dominica dreaded going home at the weekends so much that she asked me if she could stay for the weekend at my house. I had made my life seem so appealing that she wanted to experience it herself. This made me realise what a mess I had got myself into by telling lies. It was at that moment that my Mum's words came back to haunt me - "If you have done something wrong and you lie about it you will be punished much more than if you owned up to doing it in the first place."

I had two choices: I could think of a good reason why she couldn't come, but that might make her think that I didn't want her to come which wasn't the case at all. Or I could tell her the truth and that I had been lying. After days of deliberation, I decided I had no option other than to come clean and tell her the truth. I kept waiting for the right moment which never seemed to come. With all this on my mind I couldn't concentrate, and Dominica picked up on this. She asked me if anything was wrong as I was so quiet and distant, and she wondered if she had done anything to upset me. Thank goodness she noticed, because that opened the door for me to tell her everything. I thought she would be angry and disappointed and wouldn't want to be friends with me anymore, but she understood why I had lied. Then she opened up to me and told me how unhappy she was, even though she was always smiling. She hated boarding at school and didn't fit in with the other boarders, with all their pranks and games. She'd lie on the bed and read which was her way of escaping the pain of being away from home. But when she was at home, she didn't like being there either; she always felt her parents didn't want her as they never spent much time with her. She was very lonely and isolated. Like me, she used food to comfort herself and as a way of escape she would bury herself in books. Opening up to each other lifted a real weight off both our shoulders and made us much closer. I learned two very salient lessons that day - it is always best and easier to tell the truth and don't make assumptions by what you see on the outside.

Dominica did come and stay for the weekend - her parents were only too pleased. She had a positive and uplifting effect on us all and for the first time in ages we were all laughing and having fun. Dominica made sure my sister was not left out too, as she knew how it felt and anyway, we had plenty of time at night to catch up on grown up things when Carole was in bed. We had fish and chips with batter bits on Friday and on Saturday Dad took us all to a pub which had a garden where we all had Vimto and Walker's cheese and onion crisps. Dad didn't need to be badgered to come out of the pub this time. Perhaps he was on his best behaviour, but it felt as though at last I had my old Dad back. Dominica didn't want to go home, she wanted to adopt my Dad and my sister; even when Dad did things such as passing wind, falling asleep in the chair and snoring loudly and showing her his potty that he took to bed to pee in. Dominica came to stay at our house several times, but I was never invited back to hers...

Having adopted a survival mechanism to help me fit in at school, I now had to find one to help me fit in when I got home. We lived in a small semi-detached house where most families were far from well off and who often struggled to make ends meet. With my transition to becoming a Convent pupil and attending a 'posh' school I was labelled a snob. I was the brunt of verbal as well as physical abuse. Street girls wanted to pick a fight with me, they ridiculed my uniform, talked to me in a posh accent, pulled my hat off and spat at me. Once again, I felt isolated, scared and different as I didn't fit in. I remember one particular incident when my sister and I became the target of two girls who worked at one of the factories across the road from our house. As we walked home from the bus stop, they would be coming out of the factory and passing us to go in the opposite direction. For some reason they took a dislike to us, especially my sister who was very overweight due to comfort eating. Bear in mind these girls were working, so would have been 15 or 16 at least whereas I was 11 and my sister was only 9. Every time they saw us, they would call us names and tease us, but we just put our heads down, ignored them and carried on walking. This worked until one day when they called us names my sister answered them back. Well, that was it! They both approached my sister and pushed her so hard she fell into the middle of the road and landed on her wrist which I could clearly see was broken. They just went off laughing whilst I helped her up; when I looked more closely, I could see she had broken her wrist very badly as the bone was sticking out. She was crying and inconsolable not just because she was in so much pain but because of the whole situation and what had happened. Neither of us could make sense of it as we had never done anything to those girls. I was so upset for my sister as she was always being teased and bullied because of her weight. I was always being teased because I was 'posh' and so I blamed myself for her being picked on by these two as it could have been me that they were targeting. The fact that she stuck up for herself and answered back made her an easy victim as she was younger than me and more vulnerable. I tried hard to console her and make her feel better by telling her I would look after her, she would be fine and not to worry, whilst at the same time trying to look calm and in control despite the fact that I was worried stiff. When we got home, Dad was not there as he usually got home from work shortly after us. I can't remember who or how someone called an ambulance, but I think I told one of our nice neighbours who had a phone. I know we went to hospital on our own, but the rest is a blur. I do remember being at the hospital where my sister had to have her bone set - and I think they let me stay with her while she was anesthetized, and her wrist was put in a plaster cast. I am not totally sure of all the details as much of it is sketchy. When we got home, Dad was waiting; he was worried sick and when we told him what had happened, he insisted on calling the police. We didn't want him to, as we were scared of repercussions, but he told us we would be safe as the police would make sure it didn't happen again. That night my sister was still upset and in pain; her wrist was burning hot, and she was crying so much that I got in bed beside her, put my arm around her and stayed with her all night. She couldn't sleep and neither could I, but we had each other, and we were safe.

The following day the police met us off the school bus in a patrol car and we had to wait until the two perpetrators came out of the factory. We then had to identify them; they were arrested and put in the patrol car while we got out. I have never seen anyone look so scared - well now they knew how we had felt every day when we'd had to face them. Needless to say, they never targeted us again - in fact I can't ever remember seeing them again after that.

As the months passed into years, I discovered ways to fit in with the little rich girls as well as those around where we lived. As you have read, I had learned to smoke and one day at the back of the bike shed with a group of other girls, I showed them how to blow smoke rings and hold a cigarette like a film star.

Somehow, I managed to survive even though I was always in the bottom quarter of the class and was only ever an average pupil. I did my homework on time and studied hard enough for exams to get me through. After school each day I entered another world, and I became someone else. Carole and I were doing things at 13 that most people don't do until they are 18 and some stuff most people never do! We did what we liked as we had little or no supervision and as long as we were careful the neighbours didn't see us, we were okay.

The day the Telly Man came to re-possess the TV, Carole and I were smoking in the kitchen. We thought it was the authorities come to take us away, so we chucked our cigarettes in the sink and hid behind the sofa. I think he saw us through the gap in the net curtains as the knocking became so insistent, we had to answer. I was trembling as I opened the door and Carole stood behind me trembling, too. When he said who he was and what he wanted we were relieved and upset at the same time. This has had a lasting effect on us both, especially Carole, as whenever anyone knocks hard at her door she immediately goes back to that day and panics.

At school, I was good at English, but my real passion was biology. I would have liked to have been a doctor but that was never going to happen, I was even worse at physics and chemistry than I was at maths. Even if I had been good at all three, I would never have been able to afford to go to University. So, I decided I would train as a nurse as I only needed O-levels for that. I loved biology and I had an excellent biology teacher who made lessons both enjoyable and interesting. I've always pondered on the question of which came first – the good teacher you get on with or the subject you can do well – there has to be some of I suppose. I was so good at it that I took my biology O-level one year early, at the age of 14. At last, I was good at something. I wasn't just good enough; I was more than good enough, and I knew Dad would be so proud. Only one problem: in order to take the exam one year early I would have to pay to do it. I can't remember how much, but it was more than Dad could afford, even with help. I have always been resourceful and knew the meaning of my old Dad's favourite saying, "There's more than one way to skin a cat!"

I wrote a letter to my cousin's husband who was a high-ranking officer in the R.A.F. I knew he was someone who valued education and could afford to lend me the money. In the letter I explained the situation and told him that I would pay him back as soon as I could from my Saturday job at the local dry cleaners and from working in the summer holidays. He lent me the money and told me to work hard and not to let him down. I didn't - not only did I pass the exam, but I passed with one of the highest marks I had ever earned, 85%. It seemed I had achieved against all the odds. It wasn't long before I was able to save enough to pay him back, although when I gave him the cash, he wouldn't accept it. But, some years later, an aunt tarnished the memory when she said of me that I would never have amounted to anything had he not lent me the money.

I was thirteen when I found my first real boyfriend who was sixteen. It lasted until I took my other O-levels at fifteen when I caught him kissing my best friend and found out that he'd been seeing her as well as me, providing me with yet another experience to notch up on my evidence tally of "not being good enough"!

As my life has unfolded, I have realised I am not so different to anyone else. I've learned to accept disappointments and tribulations as part of growing up, as most of us go through ups and downs in life. When we are young, we think the world revolves around us and everything lasts forever - but only time is everlasting.

* * *

Chapter 3
MY STORY
Part Three

Off to Work I Go...

Even though I was hopeless at maths and didn't even pass my arithmetic proficiency, after leaving school I ended up working in a bank!

In addition to the Biology, I'd passed a year earlier, I only managed to gain a further three O-levels - in English, Religious Studies and Art. I needed five to be considered for nurse training, but I didn't care as I had changed my mind. My social life needed funding along with my smoking habit; what I earned on a Saturday at the dry cleaners was not enough for going out and drinking, especially when ten shillings of my thirty shillings pay went on bus fares and lunch. So, I decided I would leave school and work in the hosiery factory, just like my friend Karen whose house I had pretended was mine. She hadn't stayed on at school to take her O-levels, she'd left at 15 to take a job at the hosiery factory across the road from where we lived. She'd been there for over a year and was earning what seemed like a fortune. She could always afford new clothes and the latest records, going out and about whenever she liked. She only worked from 9-5 and didn't have to get up early or travel as the factory was only over the road. I'd wanted to leave school when she did, but Dad persuaded me to stay on and take my O-levels.

However, one of the girls at the Convent was the daughter of a local bank manager who needed to replace someone in the typing pool as one of his typists was soon to go on maternity leave. He asked the nuns if there was anyone they could recommend. As well as being good at Biology, I'd become proficient at shorthand and typing – another of the benefits of a private school education, they teach useful subjects too! I'd managed to pass all my exams reaching good speeds and a good level of accuracy in both. The nuns put me forward because I met the criteria, lived locally and could easily get to work by bus. Having made up my mind I was going to work in the factory, I went for the interview anyway as I didn't want to let them down or appear ungrateful. When I met the bank manager, he told me the girl who was pregnant had said she didn't expect to come back once she'd had the baby and he was now looking for a permanent replacement. Not only that, he told me his PA, who also managed the typing pool, was due to retire in a few years; there was a golden opportunity, if I was offered the job, to progress to a long and successful career with the bank. Although I wouldn't be earning as much as I would in the factory, and I would have to travel every day, I really liked the sound of that.   He said he would write and let me know if I had been successful.   I couldn't wait to get home and tell Dad, who didn't want me in a dead-end job, he would be so proud if I worked in a bank. I was on tenterhooks until the envelope with the bank logo on it arrived.   I was scared as I opened it and started to read the usual, "Thank you for attending an interview for the typist's position…"

And there, at the end of the first sentence, "… and I am pleased to tell you that you have been successful." How excited we all were - Dad, Carole and also Auntie Evelyn when she came as usual the following Wednesday. We celebrated with cake and some sparkling wine.   My other two aunts, Mum's sister and sister-in-law, were also delighted, proclaiming that if my Mum had been alive, she would have been delighted, too.

But things didn't quite turn out as expected; the girl who was pregnant lost her baby and decided to come back to work.   I thought I would be surplus to requirements, but the bank manager said he was pleased with my work and would I like to stay on - but instead of a typist as a bank clerk, with more opportunities to progress.   I stayed in the bank for six years progressing from machine room operator to cashier then on to standing orders and finally I reached the dizzy heights of being in charge of enquiries!   Who knows what I would have achieved if I had stayed? But with my lack of qualifications and my inability to do maths, I doubt if I would have made it to bank manager!

So, that is how I came to be a bank clerk without O-level maths!   I'll never forget the time my ex-maths teacher came in to cash a cheque. The look on her face when she saw me was priceless, and she must have counted her money at least three times to make sure I'd got it right!

I remember my sixteenth birthday so well; it was a milestone - as if the weight of the world had been lifted off my shoulders - because I could no longer be taken into care.   I was free at last and seemed to have so much more energy.

Dad brought a new friend home from the pub during that summer.   He was in his thirties and very trendy, with a good job, totally different to the usual people Dad befriended and brought home. He was a Chief Bonus and Quantity Surveyor who had been headhunted from his job in London by a company near to us. I liked him straight away - even more when I discovered he was divorced and had gone to court to gain custody of his two daughters, aged 6 and 10. He'd had to show that he could take care of them, just like Dad had done for us. Whilst in the area he'd met and befriended a retired couple who said they'd be delighted to look after his children until he came home from work; they wrote a letter to the Court to that effect, and everything was put in place.

Although his children were happy with each other I could sense that they missed their mum. I'd had no choice but to accept that I would never see my Mum again, so I knew what that felt like - but knowing your mum is out there somewhere brings its own level of loss. Over the summer and into the autumn he became a regular visitor. We became close and he invited me out with him and the girls at weekends. He was well educated, having been to boarding school, well dressed and confident with plenty of money and a brand-new sporty car. He spent all his spare time with the children, and they seemed like a happy family. As time went on, I grew fonder of him, and the children and he became fonder of me. I started to see them in the evenings as well as at weekends and so it progressed to staying overnight and at weekends too. We were both lost souls of a sort, so it was inevitable that a relationship would develop. I moved in with them permanently when I reached eighteen and thought I knew my own mind. When I was twenty-one, we got married and although Dad was not pleased, he accepted it, as he saw that I was happy - and for a while we were. But, because I was there to look after the children, he visited the pub more and more and it wasn't long before I realised that he was just like my Dad – an alcoholic. I tried hard to change him, and he promised to change his ways; he did for a while, but as is so often the case he became deceitful, coming home late from work and becoming more and more aggressive if I challenged him. After another couple of years walking on eggshells, I knew I had no choice but to go. So, after five years of marriage we split up.

Around that time, I saw a small two-bedroomed end-terraced house for sale in the same village where my sister lived. The house had been repossessed and the bank were looking for a quick sale. That was all well and good, but I needed a mortgage and with no deposit and no savings that was going to be very difficult, if not impossible. I hadn't told anyone apart from my closest friends that my husband and I were splitting up. A friend at the bank suggested I ask the manager about a mortgage. I was uncomfortable about that as it would mean baring my soul to him and I didn't like him much as he didn't seem very approachable. Stark necessity being the mother of courage, I forced myself to ask if he could spare me some time as there was a matter I needed to discuss. He was intrigued and took me by surprise by saying, "Shall we do it now?" I was nervous, stammering and stuttering with my heart beating ten to the dozen. I was sure he would turn me down, but I asked anyway. He was very understanding and worked out a way it could be done. He said it would be tight to start with, but I could always get someone to share with me if things got too tough. After that I saw him in a totally different light.

I came out of his office as if I were dancing on air and rang the estate agent straight away. The house was on the market for £18,500.00. I thought about offering £17,000.00 and talked it through with my sister who said, "Offer them £15,000.00, you can always increase it if they say no." They didn't say no and a few weeks later I was moving into my own little house with a few sticks of furniture and an old mattress for a bed all begged and borrowed off friends and family.

I could have asked for a settlement when I left my husband, which would have made my life much easier, but I didn't want to do that because of the children. So, all I took were my clothes and my sewing machine which all fitted very nicely in the back of my little Mini.

I found it a real struggle to make ends meet but as often happens, a timely opportunity presented itself which made life better. A friend at work had also split up from her husband; she'd moved back in with her parents and it wasn't working out.
When I broached the subject, she thought it was an excellent idea and within a couple of weeks she'd moved in with me. Thus, began one of the

happiest times of my life. Chris was calm and confident, taking everything in her stride while nothing seemed to faze her. She was practical too and could turn her hand to anything, unlike me! DIY, cooking, home décor and maintenance - you name it she could do it and do it well. With the extra money I now had, I was able to save a bit and we both started to go out and socialize more. Every Friday evening after we had done the weekly shop, we would treat ourselves either to a meal out or a takeaway. We tried somewhere different every week, places where there were offers on like BOGOF and we enjoyed the different experiences, some more than others, it has to be said! On free weekends, we'd visit country parks, National Trust houses and a cinema or the theatre. When her divorce settlement came through and it was time to move on, she bought a house just across the road! We have been the best of friends ever since.

One day, another friend, Sue, spotted an advert for ground staff in the local paper placed by Orion, a new airline which was to start operating from East Midlands Airport - only thirty minutes away. When the paperwork arrived a few days later it was a dual application form for both cabin and ground staff, everything was the same except you had to tick a box which said, "Are you applying for cabin staff or ground staff?" Applying for cabin crew had not even crossed our minds as we didn't feel we looked the part or had any relative experience, but we both ticked the cabin staff box anyway. A few weeks later I received a letter inviting me to attend an interview on 25 January 1980. I was excited to share the news with Sue, as I was sure we'd be going to the interview together. But Sue had not been asked, so I said that I would decline their offer. Sue said I should go, and she was very happy for me - how different from my convent school memory where I lost a friend by succeeding where she had failed. For Sue and me, our friendship became stronger.

But I had a problem that could prevent me from going to the interview. I was covered in psoriasis, almost from head to foot. It had flared up after my Dad had been taken into hospital where he'd nearly died of sepsis and was getting worse by the day. I was able to cover most of it up at the bank as the manager had made an exception by allowing me to wear trousers and I always wore a long-sleeved blouse. (Women wearing trousers to work was unheard of then.) Who would want to see a cabin crew member covered in scales? It was early December, and the interview was not until mid-January, so in theory there was time for it to get better.

But it didn't get better, and I was admitted to hospital on New Year's Eve. I was very depressed by this stage as not only did I look awful, but I felt awful too. Psoriasis is an autoimmune disease where your body continually regenerates skin at a faster rate than it should, and you end up with too much skin which forms unsightly scales. It itches like mad, and you try to resist scratching it but, in the end, it gets too much. You scratch only to make it bleed and crack which is not only very sore, but layers of skin fall off leaving a trail all over the floor or in the bed. To add to the torture your body cannot regulate its temperature, so if it's hot you can't sweat and cool down and if it's cold you just can't get warm. All of this affects you both physically and mentally and many people who have psoriasis to this degree will suffer from depression too. Even though it was New Year's Eve it was a huge relief to know something would be done as I couldn't go on like that any longer. I would be out of view of the public who couldn't help staring and no one would judge me because being scaly and ill in hospital is okay. I was in hospital for two weeks undergoing a strict regime of lanolin baths followed by coal tar baths, which smelt awful. This was followed by ultra-violet light treatment, which I called my National Health suntan, in conjunction with medication to slow the skin's renewal rate. After two weeks of this all the scaling had gone, although there were red marks where it had been, and I was allowed home. I was still on anti-depressants, but now I was feeling better the doctor agreed to me coming off them by gradually reducing the dose. I bought some thick tights to hide my legs and I chose a brightly coloured long sleeved blouse to go under my "interview suit." Once I had done my hair and put on some make up, even I thought I looked quite good.

The interview was one of the worst career experiences I have ever had to go through. Three people in uniform sitting before me at a desk, firing questions at me one after the other, leaving me very little time to think of an appropriate response. I was reminded of when I was a child, after mum had died, when my neighbour did exactly the same thing, trying to catch me out. I felt anxious and my mouth was dry, but I managed to answer all their questions. Then they gave me a piece of paper with a French PA announcement on it and asked me to read it aloud. On the interview form I'd ticked the box that asked if I spoke French! I did speak French but very badly and I hadn't passed my French O-Level. My accent was appalling, like something out of "Allo, Allo!" and I'm sure one of the panel tried to hide a smile.

The interview eventually came to an end, I was told I could leave, and they would write to me within two weeks to let me know their decision. I thanked them all, shook their hands and breathed a sigh of relief that it was over. I felt I hadn't done very well, but it was some consolation to know that I had got that far.

However, the interviewers had more faith in me than I had in myself and a few weeks later I began my career as an Air Hostess with British Midland Airways.

*   *   *

Chapter 4
MY STORY
Part Four

Flying High

My induction into British Midland Airways was a three-week Cabin Crew Training Course. That was another shock to the system. Most of the people on the course were glamorous, perfectly groomed with full make up, nails manicured and painted to match their lipstick. This did not apply to the male trainee stewards; I hasten to add! After introducing ourselves to each other, it became clear that most of them had always wanted to be an Air Hostess. Again, I had the feeling of not fitting in as I had never given it a thought until I'd first read the application form. You may be seeing a pattern in my life by now…

I was drawn to a lovely person on the course called Celia. She was tall, slim, blond, very pretty, and immaculately dressed with her hair in a perfect French pleat. She was a style icon and looked just the way I would like to look. She had previously been a beauty consultant in a large department store in Nottingham and she gave off an air of confidence while seeming to take everything in her stride. But, after we became friendly, she confided in me that she too felt she was out of her depth. You never can tell what's going on under the surface with people you meet in life.

At each exam, of which there were at least two per week, you had to achieve a minimum of 85% to pass. If you didn't pass you had one more chance to re-sit. Fail on that and your contract was terminated with immediate effect. The pressure was immense, but Celia and I worked our socks off and I am pleased to say we passed all of our exams on the first attempt.

Writing this and re-reading it, it looks as though I'm a glutton for punishment, or at least rather remiss when thinking things through. Anyone with an ounce of forethought would have realised that a fear of heights and working on an airline might present a problem at some stage. Jumping onto an inflatable slide from a great height and at great speed was not something I was going to relish! Fortunately, it had to be done so quickly I had very little time to think about it - I took a leap of faith and it paid off. The simulation in Long Eaton's swimming pool where we had to jump in and inflate our life jackets and then inflate and climb onto a dingy was a piece of cake after that!

The pressure in the classroom was then exchanged for even more pressure on the aircraft in the form of training flights. We were each rostered with a Line Trainer who shadowed us making sure we stuck to all the rules and regulations and that we were familiar with all the equipment on the aircraft - where it was located, how to use it and that we were able to carry out the inflight service to a high standard. My training flights were over within three weeks, and I then became part of the operating crew. As a new crew member, I was very slow, which put pressure on the rest of the crew. I was always in the wrong place at the wrong time, and nothing seemed to go smoothly. I didn't enjoy it at all. Whenever I bumped into others who had been on my training course, they were upbeat, telling me they were really loving it. It seemed everyone I met was enjoying it except me. Again, the self-doubt of not being good enough was screaming at me.

It was a few weeks later that I bumped into Celia, she was finishing a flight and I was taking over from her. I asked how she was getting on and to my surprise she felt exactly the same as me. Always in the wrong place at the wrong time, feeling that she was under every one's feet and slowing everyone down. Whenever I find a kindred struggler, just like me, I no longer feel alone. It wasn't long after that, that everything fell into place and we both began to thoroughly enjoy the job.

I loved working for British Midland in those early days, the people and the camaraderie were second to none. It was hard working to unforgiving timetables, but it was enjoyable, satisfying and rewarding and every day was different. The airline was expanding rapidly, quadrupling its size in five years, and there were lots of senior positions that needed filling. I rose through the ranks starting with No.2 stewardess in charge of the bar, then No.1 Stewardess in charge of the aircraft, followed by Line Trainer, Classroom Trainer, Deputy Fleet Stewardess, Fleet Stewardess and Regional Manager Europe until I finally reached the dizzy heights of Cabin Crew Manager, responsible for 12 European bases, 800 cabin crew and a budget of £1 million.   Not bad for someone who failed her maths O-level and was never going to be good enough to amount to anything!

But all of these positions came with their own challenges and with no experience I had to learn on the job. My best never felt good enough and with that came the stress of self-doubt. With each promotion came more work, more stress and "politics". I was always tired and often when I got home from work, I would just fall asleep as I was so exhausted. This became the norm, and in order to cope I resorted to my old faithful – comfort eating. Chips, chocolate, sweets, biscuits and crisps became my diet which made the situation worse. At some point in my airline career, I took a step back and realised that it was a younger person's occupation, and I would be wise to look at getting a qualification to give me more options for when I left.   So, I started to study for an Open University Degree in Psychology.

About this time, I began my relationship with Ahmed. He was very good looking - he had charisma, charm and was very intelligent.   Everyone liked him. While we lived together, he was working at the Leicester Royal Infirmary with lots of attractive nurses and I felt very insecure. Not feeling good enough and worrying that he would find someone better than me just added to my stress. I always had a gut feeling that he was seeing someone else, but I didn't really want to find out.

Then one day, out of the blue, he said he was leaving me and going to live in a flat in Leicester. He blamed me, saying I was too possessive and that he needed his own space.   I hadn't seen that coming and I felt so distraught that I even rang the Samaritans, believing yet again that there was something wrong with me. I felt desperate, worthless, and that there was no point in going on. After talking to the Samaritans, I felt a lot better.

I then tried to make an appointment with a psychiatrist and found you have to get a referral from your GP. The thought of going to my doctor and telling her about all of this filled me full of dread. Despite my fears, the doctor was so nice and understanding that I broke down and cried uncontrollably. She made me realise it wasn't all my fault and she recommended counselling - which I hadn't considered.

Counselling helped me to understand that the sexual abuse I'd suffered was not my fault and that the failed relationships were not totally my fault either. This helped, but I knew I wanted more answers, so I paid to see a psychologist who had previously been a psychiatrist. I went every week for two years and although both of these therapies helped me to cope with the symptoms neither of them did anything to help me deal with the cause. It was later on in my healing journey that I discovered EFT and it was this that changed my life completely. (See more about this in the resources chapter).

However, in the meantime, I had consciously and subconsciously decided no more relationships for me, they were too painful. So, I spent the next 22 years on my own.

In the final year of my degree, I was faced with the airline company restructuring and all four of the Cabin Services management team had to apply for the jobs. I applied for my own job - Cabin Services Manager. Being in limbo while waiting was something I couldn't cope with at all well.   I need to know, then I can plan, and I now know why. It stems from the time when I would come home from school not knowing whether or not Mum had died. The not knowing can feel more stressful than the actual outcome.

In the middle of all of this I was called up for Jury Service which took me away for two weeks at a most critical time.   Upon my return I was told I hadn't got the job and would be demoted. I couldn't understand it as I had been doing the job; not only that, but I had also been told I was doing a good job and that the interview was just a formality.   The person who got the job was the only male applicant and was the least experienced of all of us. Thankfully, I was in the final year of my OU studies, and it wouldn't be long before I had gained my degree and could leave to take up a new career.

Meanwhile, I resolved to work with the new manager, to help and support him, sharing my own experience for him to be successful in his new role. Instead of seeing me as an asset, he saw me as a threat and, along with the other two managers, they went out of their way to make my life almost impossible. If I entered the office and they were talking, it would go quiet; they would often go into another office to talk together, excluding me. I was given tasks that were impossible to achieve and a workload that was impossible to complete. It was dreadful. I felt isolated, alone, excluded and desperate. I didn't know what to do. Every day I felt sick in my stomach as I dreaded going to work and each day, I couldn't wait to get home, collapse on the sofa exhausted and then comfort eat until it was time to go to bed. I thought I could stick it out for another few months until I got my degree, but after several weeks I became ill and didn't go to work. After a few days of turmoil in my head I decided I wasn't ever going back, and I left a message to that effect. I was at the end of what I could cope with. I had a lot to lose - my job, my company car and I was also on my own with a mortgage and bills to pay. I had learned to be careful, and I had some savings but that wouldn't keep me going for long. My peers and colleagues at the airline all thought I was being forced out and declared it was unfair dismissal. That was an enormous boost to my morale because I'd started to think that the problem was me. The HR department left me messages to call them, but I couldn't face the conflict; all I wanted to do was switch off, and that's what I did. For several days I just slept all day, not even eating.

The injustice of it all made me angry, so I made the decision to take them to court on the grounds of unfair dismissal. I filled in all the paperwork to have my case heard and the hearing was scheduled for three days at Leicester Magistrates Court. I was defending myself as I couldn't afford a solicitor.

One morning, when I was in the midst of preparing all my paperwork, Carole called me to say her husband had just died. It hit me like a bomb dropping - I just couldn't believe it. I stopped what I was doing and rushed over to her house to witness the most bizarre scene. My sister, who worked as a carer, had laid her dead husband on the floor where she had washed him and dressed him in clean blue pyjamas. She was in shock and was now on autopilot doing what she had done many times in the past when an elderly client died. I didn't know until later that she had found her husband still alive and begging for help; she'd tried to save his life by giving him mouth to mouth resuscitation, but it hadn't worked. I didn't know what to do, so I just bent down and put my arms around her. While all this was going on her elder son arrived home, saw his dad dead on the floor and just went straight upstairs as he too couldn't come to terms with what he was seeing. The rest is mostly a blur. I remember that, after the body had been collected, we had to go and break the news to her younger son who was still at school. When we told him, he shrieked, screamed and sobbed uncontrollably. It broke my heart and still does every time I think about it. One day they were a happy family and the next they were broken; things would never be the same again. Never more relevant than at that time was the saying, "Live every day to the full, tomorrow might be too late."

I couldn't sleep. I was doing all I could for Carole and her boys but cannot describe the emotions that were surging through my whole being. Nevertheless, my case was due to be held in a few days' time. My sister had previously offered to come with me so that I didn't have to face it alone but that wasn't going to happen now - I couldn't let her go through all that. Then I thought of asking my friend Kate who was a legal secretary. She was very organized, very capable and would know the ropes. She said yes and I really don't know what I would have done without her. She organised and referenced the paperwork, passing it to me at the right page when I was questioning them. She was unflappable, which calmed me down and she boosted me when I needed it. She was brilliant and I cannot thank her enough. The three days were stressful and tiring and I couldn't think straight, but I kept going. I lost the case, but I'm not surprised given the circumstances and the fact that I was way out of my depth. There was just me and Kate up against those Goliaths: their HR Director, teams of assistants and the very best in solicitors. I was disappointed but, now it was over, at least I had closure and could move on. As I was leaving the court, their solicitor came over to me and shook my hand; he told me that I should have won the case. He said I would definitely have done so if I'd been represented by a solicitor. I cannot tell you how much that meant to me; my underlying belief of not being good enough and that there was something wrong with me had almost convinced me yet again that I was the problem.

After the case I felt relieved, a lot lighter and clear headed. I felt responsible for my newly widowed sister and realised I needed to get a job quickly, before my savings ran dry.

In my search for a job, I came across an advert in the Sunday Times: Consultancy Network Associates (CNA) were looking for self-employed management consultants. For a fee they provided a four-day training course with access to a network of other consultants, together with marketing support and back up. I decided to apply but, even though I had the skills, I didn't think I would be accepted as I didn't feel I was good enough - again! Consultancy Network Associates had been started by Robert who then took on a partner Albert. Robert's background was consultancy and Albert's was executive recruitment. Shortly after I joined, Albert decided the time was right to set up an Executive Search arm and he approached several of the management consultants who he thought might be interested in becoming Executive Search franchisees. I was one of them. Of course, I was interested, as this was an opportunity not just to earn a living but to build a business which I could sell down the line. After a few months building my Executive Search business, Robert decided to retire, and Albert asked me if I would consider joining CNA as he needed help to grow the network. I was there for 15 years, became a shareholder and together we built a very successful business. CNA Executive Search was bought in 2009 by Pertemps and at the time of writing is still operating successfully today.

For those of you who are self-employed you will know how much goes into building a successful business. You have to be focused and prepared to work 24/7 with virtually no time off. You have to manage people, premises and finances, all on a shoestring and the responsibility and worry of it all is very stressful. This was when stress really started to affect me seriously. I was always tired and every muscle and joint ached. Everything was an effort, and I was constantly having to push myself to keep going. I tried to eat healthily but as I often didn't get home until mid-evening and didn't have the energy to cook, I relied on quick and easy processed food or take away meals and I was still comfort eating, too. I became run down and caught a very nasty virus. I couldn't take time off and eventually, after pushing myself to keep going at work, I collapsed. It was very scary, and I thought there was something seriously wrong with me. Despite my protests, Albert took me straight to the doctor where I was told that as a result of pushing myself too hard for too long, my body had completely shut down. I was advised to take at least 6 months off to recover and with that I went home, collapsed on the sofa and there I stayed pretty much for 6 weeks. I didn't have the energy to do anything. For the first and only time in my life I really couldn't have cared less about anything; I completely shut down, just needing to rest. It took a long time for me to feel well enough to return to work, initially on a part-time basis then gradually building up to full time. However, I was still not well, and I always felt so tired. Instead of getting better these symptoms continued until, after a few months, I was so concerned that I went to the doctor again where I had every blood test you can think of which all came back with normal results. I wanted to know what could possibly be causing these symptoms if there was nothing physically wrong.

The Doctor said, "Stress."

Well, at least now I had a diagnosis, but I didn't know what I could do about it as I had a stressful job, lived on my own and had to do everything myself. This was when I started my research in earnest, focussing on stress and its effects on both body and mind.

And there you have the potted version of My Story and, if you like, this has been my own Onion Therapy. I have stripped back the layers that were growing year after year, relationship after relationship, trauma after trauma.

We cannot know what effect the conflict and stress of living has on our ability to cope. We react to things - often in inappropriate and unrelated ways that seem to bear no relationship to either the cause or the symptom. The answers are often to be found when we go back to uncover the very first time that we tried to cope with something we didn't understand, and which caused us stress.

I now know that living in a continual state of stress and on high alert has a major impact on our physical, mental, emotional and spiritual health. It prevents us from being truly happy and enjoying life to the full. By working on my own issues and working with others on theirs, I have seen how both health and quality of life can be improved. You see it is my belief that most, if not all illnesses, including cancer, are to some degree a result of stress. Whether that is physical, mental, emotional or a combination of all of them, I have realised it is not so much the situation we are in that is stressful but the way we feel about it. The bad news is most of the time we cannot change the situation, the good news is we can always change the way we feel about it.

Often, we are taught how to feel, second hand, by our parents when we are young. What we believe and how we feel and respond comes from our sub-conscious mind - our other than conscious mind - as some call it. Our sub-conscious mind will react almost instantly, and its purpose is to protect us and keep us safe, keep us alive, keep us breathing. But sometimes it needs a bit of re-training – as mine did...

*   *   *

Jesus Appears to Thomas:
24 Now Thomas, one of the Twelve, was not with the disciples when Jesus came.
25 So the other disciples told him, "We have seen the Lord!"
But he said to them, "Unless I see the nail marks in his hands and put my finger where the nails were, and put my hand into his side, I will not

believe."

26 A week later his disciples were in the house again, and Thomas was with them. Though the doors were locked, Jesus came and stood among them and said, "Peace be with you!"

27 Then he said to Thomas, "Put your finger here; see my hands. Reach out your hand and put it into my side. Stop doubting and believe."

28 Thomas said to him, "My Lord and my God!"

29 Then Jesus told him, "Because you have seen me, you have believed; blessed are those who have not seen and yet believed."

John 20:24-29

Chapter 5

Who Are You?

You have read my story and how my experiences not only impacted on my health, but my whole life. I'll tell you in this chapter what strategies and therapies I used and how they worked for me, but that doesn't necessarily mean they will work for you; one size does not fit all. It's the same with treating illnesses - and cancer is one example of that. No one individual has the same genetic make-up, the same life experiences or the same beliefs as another. There will be similarities but not everything can be the same. Even identical twins evolve differences as they grow older. It therefore makes sense to tailor everything, health-wise, to the individual. Currently however, conventional medicine doesn't do that. In order to tailor a health program that is unique to you, you need information so that you can make informed choices. At the end of this book, you will find direction to some excellent books and websites. There are hundreds of others out there, but these I can wholly recommend for health in general and cancer in particular. Access to information is the start but, in most cases, we do nothing with it. Have you ever bought a book and not even read it? Self-help books that you have read, but not got around to implementing any of the things that you know will make a difference to your health.   Have you ever wondered why that is?

I am going to introduce you now to someone you will know very well. He's been around since Biblical times – his name is Doubting Thomas. He is that little nagging voice who casts doubt on anything he isn't used to or has not come across before, or a bad experience he doesn't want to repeat, and he is partly to blame here.   This really is the core of the issue and the primary reason for the name of this book.

Every conscious and subconscious action (habit, auto-emotion, response and so on) is in some degree conditioned by what you have been brought up to and influenced to believe. Most of our beliefs – those things we consider to be true – are good for us and allow us to survive and thrive; in some cases, they really do empower us. But some of them are out of date. As children we were cocooned in all sorts of magical and mysterious falsehoods – Santa Claus, the tooth fairy or the bogeyman for example. We grew out of them of course and now see them for what they are. But remember back to when you absolutely believed them and how fast you learned not believe in the falsehood anymore and move on with your life. Well, no harm was done by these benign little critters, but there are lots more little beliefs, layers if you like, that make up our day-to-day modus operandi and some of them, even though they may be out of date, are still clogging up our lives and stopping us moving forward or changing for the better. Our friend Tom is the custodian of these limiting beliefs and perhaps he wasn't paying attention when the evidence to disprove the belief was first aired. If your beliefs are limiting you, just as they were me, it would be a good idea to change them, and I am going to show you how. But first you need to identify them – peel back the layers if you like - and when you have and have then learned how to change them and make them work for you, not only will your health improve but your whole life will improve too - I promise you that.

Life can be dangerous and so inside us all is a mechanism that is there to keep us safe - this is often referred to as our subconscious mind. This operates automatically, out of our conscious awareness, and is always running in the background. Most of the time we are not aware of it. We don't have to remember to breathe or to make sure our heart keeps on beating, it just happens automatically and will continue to do so throughout our lives, unless it becomes faulty. But the subconscious mind not only protects us physically, but it also protects us mentally and emotionally too.

Here is an example of how the subconscious gets programmed: If, when you were a child, your mother screamed and ran away from spiders you will have learned that spiders are dangerous and that will have been programmed into your subconscious mind. From then on, whenever you see a spider, you will automatically respond as if it is dangerous, and your subconscious mind will send signals to your physical body to prepare for 'fight or flight'. As you grow older you realise that most spiders are harmless and there is no need to be scared of them. However, your subconscious mind has been hard-wired to keep you safe and will continue to believe that spiders are dangerous so you will have a fear (phobia) of them for the rest of your life. The way to change this response is to reprogram it and this book will show you ways and techniques to enable you to change those beliefs that are limiting you.

Here's a real-life example that is used in modern day change management therapy, thousands of times every year, and it works – permanently. Bad habits which are labelled addictions, such as smoking, are tough to give up. If you have ever been a smoker you will know - and Tom knows it's nigh on impossible, so he will make sure your conscious mind is absolutely aware that giving up is not worth thinking about. He also understands that beliefs might not be for ever - like believing in Santa Clause. If you ask Tom to consider visiting the Museum of Old Beliefs, where Santa resides along with the tooth fairy and where there may be space for a few more, he will like this. You see, Tom doesn't like letting go of a belief for ever, but he is okay if, now and again, he can go back and visit it in the future; he is, after all, very loyal. In this Museum of Old Beliefs, we could ask Tom if he would help you move on in your life by putting a current belief – the belief that it is hard to stop smoking – into a glass case so that we can go back and visit it if we need to. He likes metaphors, so this belief could be in the form of a packet of your favourite cigarettes. This works better if you get a practitioner to guide you through the process, such as a hypnotherapist, a smoking cessation consultant, or an EFT therapist. There are a number of other factors at play when giving up something like smoking but, when the time is right for you, this is the technique that persuades the likes of Tom to let go and this could be the difference that makes all the difference, as it has thousands of times. Over the last twenty years millions of people have given up smoking. It really cannot be that hard can it, Tom? Of course, I have oversimplified this to make the point, and the point is this: it is often the belief that it is hard, that makes it hard in the first place. Translate this scenario into any one of dozens of other changes you'd like to make in your life – going to the gym, slimming classes, breathing properly, learning something new and so on – and you have the possibility of changing your life for good, for ever...

So, let's go back to the very beginning to see how it all started and how we acquired our beliefs: At the very heart of us all is our core self - that is who we are. When we are born, we are a blank slate, a genetically unique being with genes from each of our parents. But it is not our genetic makeup that defines who we are - that only accounts for about 1% according to Bruce Lipton Ph.D.—it is the environment we grow up in. This is a fundamental change in approach to healing, as in his book "The Biology of Belief" he scientifically proves and dispels the theory that if your parents and close relatives have had cancer then you are going to get it. There may be 1% of your genes that are indicative of the cancer, but it is your environment that will determine whether you actually get it or not. This is the basis of the new science of Epigenetics which revolutionises the understanding of the link between mind and matter and the profound effects it has on our personal lives and the collective life of our species. So, who we are is 1% genetic and the rest is what we learn (absorb) from our environment, and this predominantly determines who we are, how we live our lives and what we do or don't achieve.

As we grow and develop, we build layers to protect that core. Ask yourself: Who are you? Over the years you may have lost sight of who you are by trying to conform in order to fit in, or you might adapt and change your views on the way you think and feel because you are afraid of not being liked or being criticised. Are you someone who is trying so hard to meet other people's expectations that you compromise your own?   Have you lost sight of your true identity by trying to be the perfect parent or the perfect manager, the perfect employee and doing things that you believe you ought to be doing even when it doesn't feel natural? Are you afraid of letting people see who you really are, because there are things you have done which you're not proud of or feel guilty about? If that sounds like you, you are not on your own.   That was me. In fact, we all do it to varying degrees, we build layers of protection just like the layers of an onion. Peel these away and you'll find your true self, be at one with yourself and then you'll experience the real you. I have done this, and it transformed my life. When I was recently asked to make a list of what I wanted to make me happy I couldn't think of one single thing. If you had asked me 30 years ago, I would probably have said a new house, a new car, to win the lottery, a new computer, etc.   These things might have made me happy for a while, but they would have only papered over the cracks. Many people who are looking for happiness, and I was one of them, look in the wrong place.   They think material things, new relationships, having the perfect body and the like will make them happy, but it doesn't last. Once they've got what they wanted they realise they're still not happy, so they decide it's because they need something else and so on and so on. The pattern just keeps on repeating, with them never being happy no matter what.   Why?   Because the cracks re-appear. They are looking in the wrong place.   Happiness is not an external thing; it comes from within. By getting to your core, beneath those layers of protection that you've built up over the years, you will find what you really want, for you as a person. What do you get sometimes when you peel an onion? Tears! As you uncover who you are, along the way you may not like what you find.   You may have buried some of the real you and Tom keeps that lid on pretty firmly! You might not want people to know who you really are because you feel ashamed, guilty or embarrassed by some of the things you have said and done, or bad things that have happened to you throughout your life.   You might not know what you really think or be able to say what you really want to say, in case it upsets people or in case they may not like you. It can be a very scary process. This is what I have done by writing My Story; it's the first time I have ever truly opened up about what happened, and I feel exposed with no protection whatsoever. You know all about me, my innermost secrets, things I have never told anyone before.   Things I have been ashamed of and felt guilty about. I've shied away from anything that could remind me of those times all my adult life. Before I took off my layers and peeled back my truth for all to see, I worried myself sick. I had sleepless nights and stuffed myself with snacks and sweets and bad things. Tom was having a real go at me for days and days. Then, I sat down and wrote it. And do you know? I cannot believe why I was so worried and got so worked up. Now I'm not worried about it in the least!   That is a massive change for me. I'm a very private person and some of the things I have written about in this book, even my sister didn't know about.   I have only been able to do this because I have made peace with myself, I have learned to accept, respect and love myself for who I am and I can honestly say that at the age of 61, I am truly happy.   Now, when I can't think of a single thing if I ask myself what more would make me happy, it's because I've found happiness within myself.   For example, take Mike, my partner who I've been with for 9 years now, after being on my own for over 20 years: I don't need him to make me happy, but the fact that I have him in my life is the icing on the cake.   And that is just one example, there are many more.

So, peeling back the layers, learning how to reprogram your subconscious mind and to change your beliefs is the key to everything and I have called the process Onion Therapy.

*   *   *

"Man is an onion made up of a hundred integuments, a texture made up of many threads.   The ancient Asiatic's knew this well enough, and in the Buddhist Yoga an exact technique was devised for unmasking the illusion of the personality.   The human merry-go-round sees many changes: the illusion that cost India the efforts of thousands of years to unmask is the

same illusion that the West has laboured just as hard to maintain and strengthen."

Herman Hesse - Steppenwolfe

Chapter 6

The Search Begins

Since my school days when I excelled at Biology I have always been interested in health and wellbeing and have spent a lot of my spare time learning and practising how the human body works and how we can improve it, especially when things go wrong. Since 2008 my focus has been on researching cancer as well as broader health issues, and the next part of this book contains a good deal of what I have learned. Trying different approaches to diet and lifestyle made me realise that no one size fits all. Not only is it a combination of things, but it is finding the right combination for you. This can only be done if you have the information in the first place and that is what I hope to give you in this book.

When I started looking for the reasons for my ill health all those years ago, there was very little information accessible. Now, with the internet, we are awash with it, and most of it can be easily found. Although it can be very confusing, time consuming and overwhelming when you are trying to find what is right for you, it is pleasing to see that the medical profession at last have started to endorse some of the things that would have been shunned years ago. There is a shift towards complementary medicine, the focus is starting to move away from the more traditional approach of treating symptoms with pills and medication, to getting the body to utilize its own healing mechanisms to treat the cause. For instance, meditation and mindfulness as a way of managing stress was not in the mainstream years ago. However, it makes sense when even doctors agree that 90% of illnesses are caused by stress. Nowadays we are being encouraged more to eat healthily, as it has been proven that getting the right nutrition can reverse illnesses like type 2 diabetes, prevent obesity and reduce the risk of heart attacks and strokes. Even Hippocrates the founder of traditional medicine said, "Let food be thy medicine and medicine be thy food." So why is it that most doctors are only given a few hours training in nutrition?   Is there an agenda at play here?   I will come to that later. At least with activity the medical professions are recognising its importance and doing something about it, in some cases prescribing membership to gyms and slimming clubs.

All of these things, nutrition, activity and stress management, are a step in the right direction. Any one of them in isolation will make a difference to your health, put them all together and it will make a massive difference. But there are more aspects to being healthy than these three things, as I have found and you will see, and complementary therapies offer many of them. I'll start with Reflexology.   Around the time I had been so ill, and doctors couldn't find anything physically wrong, a friend introduced me to it; it involves pressing points on the feet which correspond to all the organs and glands of the body. I am an open-minded sceptic and, even though I thought this was all a bit too way out, I decided to give it a go. The first day seemed to make no difference except for the first time in years I had a good night's sleep, a deep sleep and I woke up feeling refreshed and energized. That made a big difference to me. Amazing! Just by pressing points on my feet. After a few weeks of regular treatments, my symptoms improved noticeably, and I settled into the routine of having one a month.   Although my symptoms had improved, I knew there was still more to be done. I was so impressed that shortly after my first treatment, I trained as a Reflexologist.   Although I was still working at the time, I wanted to make sure that I gained as much experience as I could and so I decided to become a volunteer therapist. That is when I came across the Cancer Self Help Group in Loughborough.

This group had been started in 1983 by two ladies both of whom had been diagnosed with terminal cancer.   In those days there were no support groups, it was taboo even to speak about cancer.   In the absence of support and information, the two ladies set up a group which met every Monday evening above a health food shop in Loughborough. Later on, it moved to John Storer House where we continue to meet to this day. This group is different. It was, and still is, ahead of its time. It is not a tea and sympathy group; it is exactly what is says on the tin: a self-help group. Members have access to information from a comprehensive library of books, audios, videos and guest speakers. They help and support each other and learn from each other's experiences. In addition, from the very beginning complementary therapies were, and still are, available to members ranging from reflexology, reiki, spiritual healing, EFT (Emotional Freedom Techniques) and various forms of massage, crystal and colour healing. Meditations and visualisations are an integral part of the healing process as is Tai Chi, Yoga and other forms of exercise. The group is not just for those who have cancer, it is for everyone, including their families, friends and carers, as well as those who want to avoid getting cancer in the first place. The two ladies who started the group outlived their given "terminal" prognosis. Gill Hurd lived a further twelve years and Joyce Walton is still alive, she is 87 and has overcome three different cancers, ovarian, mouth and bladder.

I have learned so much from Joyce, she is inspirational. I visit her every week, not just because I enjoy her company but to pick her brains to try to determine what factors make the difference between surviving cancer or dying from it. One thing I have learned, as is the case in many therapies, it is a combination of things - but beliefs play the major part. Even though Joyce was told that she was not going to survive, she didn't believe it. She told me, "Dying from cancer was never an option as I had three young boys, and one of them was such a handful I knew my husband would never be able to cope with him."

Having set up the group, others heard about it and Joyce and Gill were asked for advice and help in setting up more groups, and even travelled to Guernsey to help set up one there. Shortly after they began, they came across Dr Patrick Kingsley, a G.P. from Ibstock who treated patients using natural therapies, diet and supplements instead of medication. He worked with the group full time until his retirement but was always available afterwards for advice and to give talks. We all learned a lot from him, as well as from many members who also outlived their "terminal" prognosis.

When I started as a volunteer with the group 10 years ago, it fitted perfectly with what I had learned about health. Having the opportunity to work with people with cancer and seeing them not only survive, but thrive, using a combination of different approaches, fascinated me. I had to find out more and that has been my passion and the focus of my research since that time.

How do you keep healthy? How can you combat stress? What are the symptoms of cancer, the causes, the treatments - both conventional and complementary - why do some people survive, and some do not? Why does cancer come back for some and not for others? So many questions needing so many answers but working with different people with different cancers and those who care for people with cancer, has helped me to identify factors that seem to be important. Not only in managing, treating and healing cancer, but also in avoiding it in the first place. If I have done my job right as an author (and Steve has as my writers' coach) you will be able to draw your own conclusions from the information I will give you. Not everyone will survive cancer because all types of cancer are curable, all people are not. For Joyce, death was "not an option" for others it is. Talking about dying is just as important as talking about living, something we make a point of doing at the group. Another important thing I have learned that might surprise you, not everyone wants to get better.

There comes a time when they have had enough, they are tired and are only trying to keep going for the sake of their family, not for themselves. This is hard for their families to accept but it is important that they give them permission to die and support them once they have made their decision. Studies have shown, when seriously ill people have a "plan B" to deal with death in case they do not get better, they generally survive longer than those who do not. This is discussed further in chapter 12

Having found the benefits of reflexology I started to have regular massages with aromatherapy oils; I learned to meditate, I changed my diet, went to see a nutritionist who prescribed nutritional supplements, took up Yoga and Pilates and then I found Reiki. My Reflexologist introduced Reiki to me, describing it as a natural healing system which helps to clear blockages in the body's energy field allowing healing to take place on all three levels, physical, emotional and spiritual. I didn't understand (or believe in) the concept of spiritual healing and didn't feel comfortable with it at all but again, I tried it anyway. I researched Reiki before my first session and learned that it was a form of energy healing and the healing would go to where it was needed, not necessarily where it was wanted – more about this later. There are three levels of Reiki and for each level you need to be attuned to the energy.   Reiki level 1 enables you to treat yourself, family and friends, level 2 takes you a step further enabling you to treat paying clients and level 3 which is Reiki Master level enables you to train, mentor and attune others.   At the time I had no intention of doing anything other than level one and treating myself, but after 6 months I felt compelled to train to the second level. Reiki was a big factor in changing my life and my career; it wasn't long afterwards that we sold CNA and I started to work full time as a complementary therapist.

While the sale of the business was going through, I was introduced to the third major life changing therapy - EFT (Emotional Freedom Techniques). EFT is effective by quickly and permanently altering negative emotions, troubling thoughts and destructive behaviour patterns. Together with finding help with a long list of psychological as well as physical problems, in only 2 sessions I overcame my fear of driving.   EFT has had a massive impact on my health, physically, emotionally and spiritually and it is EFT that has enabled me to deal with, instead of cope with, the trauma of my sexual abuse, other traumas and debilitating beliefs and habits.   Not only that, but it also led me further into the field of 'Energy Healing'.

In order to understand how and why this works, it is helpful to understand what energy actually is in this context. That's a subject that deserves its own book and I cannot claim to understand the physics, but put simply, energy is what gives us the power to live.

Our bodies survive physically by converting food into energy – heat, movement, thought, regeneration of cells and so on. This sort of energy is, in the main, measurable and provable. There is another sort of energy that is harder to measure that was discovered by those giants standing on the shoulders of giants – Archimedes, Newton, Einstein, et al. It is the collective force that brings civilizations into being and it is driven by faith and belief. All the world's religions that ever were rely on this force, this unfathomable, untouchable yet overwhelmingly palpable energy. Modern thinking now refers to this as the universal life force and it is a power greater than us, something that we cannot yet explain, but we can all feel it and know it is there.

It's fair to say that energy is the universal life force that is in each and every one of us and everything in the universe. Religions can no longer hold together our communal beliefs, but they seek to further understand this power and harness its benefits. We all have the ability to feel it in our spirituality and it is separate from religion; it has more to do with what we believe, and this is the source of where our energy comes from. Spirituality is also a personal thing, and we are all unique. Some people follow a religion; there are more than 4,200 religions in the world all with faith and belief at the core of their communal connectivity. Others believe in the power of the Universe; others just refer to it as the Source. In the context of my research, it is beliefs that impact upon our ability to heal or not. Accepting the premise that we are held together entirely of energy, it makes sense to use techniques that we call "Energy Medicine" as part of our healing tool kit. Energy Medicine has its roots in Eastern cultures and is still being used to a large extent today. Like the Indian Ayurvedic System, Chinese Acupuncture (which is said to date back between 3,500 and 4000 years), Qi Gong (the foundation of Traditional Chinese Medicine (TCM), Hypnosis, Dowsing (which uses tools to allow the subconscious to answer questions) or Kinesiology (which uses muscle tension to detect the effects of thought, colour, foods and nutrients on the human energy system). More energy therapies are becoming popular today: Homeopathy, Crystal Therapy, Reflexology, Reiki and EFT are some of the most popular and some 40% of us are now turning to these. Even today's traditional healing professions are learning (or re-learning) that life is an "energy" phenomenon.   Emotions are specific forms of energy and as energy, emotions can be treated directly and simply.   This is a radical new approach for mainstream psychology medicine.

So now you know a little bit about my healing journey and the things that I have found along the way that have made a big difference to my health. There is no doubt that I have come a long way from that stressed and poorly younger me. But there's still a heck of a lot for me to learn.   It is all very well knowing the theory but putting it into practice is the hardest thing.   I will give you information on what you can do to improve your health as well as lots of tips and techniques to help you to put it into practice.

One thing is for sure though, after all is said and done, the key to winning the war on cancer and any other disease for that matter, is prevention...

*   *   *

"An ounce of prevention is worth a pound of cure."
-Benjamin Franklin

Chapter 7

Prevention IS Better Than Cure

Prevention is better than cure with most bad things in life and this is never truer than when we consider cancer. The problem is, because there are so many facets to the disease, there are so many steps to prevention. We are already near to information overload with things we have to do to survive on a daily basis - never mind reading, researching and practicing everything we are told we should do to keep healthy. Even if we do the research, there are so many contradictions that we don't know what or who to believe, so most of us take the easy way out and do nothing - or we try to do some of them. But then, life gets in the way.

I am going to make it simple.

I'll give you a variety of quick and easy techniques that take little time which can be done anywhere. I have called it 'the quick fix' - It takes less than 5 minutes, but your health could improve considerably.

But before we go to the quick fix, I'd like to explain this:
You may believe that improving your health is difficult, it takes a lot of hard work and is not much fun or there's no gain without pain and usually, when we believe something, it becomes true! This can prevent you from even starting by relying on your past experiences of failure. Beliefs play a major role in whatever we do or, more to the point, what we don't do. They are so ingrained deep down in our subconscious that we will struggle to change anything in our lives without first dealing with the limiting belief.

Onion Therapy gives you the information to make the right choice for you, together with the tools to change your beliefs, which in turn will enable you to put the information into practice. Treat the root cause of your limiting beliefs and the change you put into place will last! We are all unique. Consider our relationship with our weight: some of us are fat, some of us are thin; some of us have a problem with food in that we live to eat, others maintain a healthy weight as they eat to live. Some comfort eat to distract from other problems in life or past history, using food as a coping mechanism. I used to do this to numb my painful emotions. For those suffering from anorexia, it is a way of getting some control into their life and for others it is a combination. As well as the emotional effect eating has, it also creates physical and chemical reactions in our minds and bodies and so there are physical impulses that cause over or under-eating. This is why diets alone often won't work. We've been programmed at an early age. How many of you were told when you were a child to clean your plate and now find it very difficult to leave anything even if you are full? Or you can't leave the table until you've eaten everything, or you can't have a pudding unless you eat your dinner? As children you were given chocolate to comfort you if you injured yourself, or if you'd been good, after a visit to the doctor or (worst of all ironies) a sweet after a visit to the dentist. The bonds and beliefs that go with food run into every part of our lives. Our subconscious mind, like a stubborn old friend who never grows up and hates any change, is difficult to persuade away from that which you have always done. This stubborn old friend, who has only ever tried its best to keep you safe by using what it knows, needs new evidence to let you change. Doubting Tom refuses to change his belief until he can see and feel that the new order is safe and secure. It's no wonder then that diets often don't work in the long term.

There are many that I have tried: Weight Watchers, Slimming World, Atkins, Rosemary Conley, Low Carb, High Carb, The Cabbage Diet, The Cambridge Diet to name but a few. Why didn't they work in the long term? There's no simple answer. There are so many aspects to disorderly eating. One of the most common and most powerful reasons is the belief that when we are on a diet, we are depriving ourselves and it is therefore hard work to lose weight. You start off and lose a good few pounds right at the beginning, earning praise from your peers and yourself. But Doubting Tom will keep nagging away and, at a moment when your guard is down and you are almost hurting from hunger, Tom knows that a little snack will remove the hurt and you succumb. Then off down the slippery slope you go.

During the process of writing this book Weight Watchers have re-branded and are now called Wellness Workshops. They have worked out that if you want people to lose weight and adopt a healthy lifestyle in the long term, you need to remove the association with the word diet. That's a step in the right direction, but it is not enough. Weight Watchers operates on a points system where you are allocated a number of points to use up in food on a daily and weekly basis. Each food is allocated a set number of points. It is an easy system which is worked out on an individual basis and the points you are allowed are worked out based on your weight and how much you need to lose or to maintain your weight in the long term. There is no doubt that it works if you stick to it and even doctors are recommending it to their overweight patients, but I question how healthy it is. From a weight point of view, it will definitely help with the obesity crisis but in order to be healthy you need to eat healthily. Although Weight Watchers encourage you to make healthy choices it is still possible to eat the required number of points in chocolate, snacks, crisps, etc. and still lose weight. Slimming World is another example of a diet that works, (in the short term) but instead of a points system they have a sins system. From a psychological viewpoint they really need to change that don't you think? Doubting Tom would never call them sins!

I have used how we deal with weight issues as an example of how complex and ingrained our beliefs are and how we are all different and all unique. There is no one common factor that causes eating disorders just as there is no common factor yet identified that causes cancer or determines who will survive it. Men and women are different but cancer per se is gender neutral. Research done over 10 years ago, showed that for adult women between the ages of 25 and 75 the leading cause of death was cancer, with breast cancer the biggest killer, and this is on the increase.

In her book Your Life in Your Hands, Professor Jane Plant chronicles, in part, her own journey through 5 progressively worse episodes of breast cancer and describes how she used her training as a scientist to cope with both the disease and the treatments she was given for it. Her scientific training taught her to observe and record everything, to root out every fragment of information, to sift the relevant from the irrelevant, the rational from the irrational and to keep asking the two key questions that are at the very heart of science: why and how. Her book contains what she believes are the answers to those two questions regarding breast cancer. She also includes information about prostate cancer as she observed in her research that much of the data and information about prostate cancer leads to conclusions similar to those regarding the cause and treatment of breast cancer. Most of what she advocates focuses on a change of diet which she calls The Plant Program. There are suggestions on how, by changing values, behaviour patterns and improving our environment, we can reduce our exposure as a society to some of the factors which may contribute to these diseases. Using this program, Jane cleared herself of cancer and she details this in her book, together with case studies of others who have done the same.

So, to 'the quick fix'. (Are you listening Tom?)

The first step you need to do to improve your health is to adjust your posture by standing up straight. This is something I can remember always being told to do as a child, but I didn't realise then how important good posture is and how poor posture can lead to health problems. If you slouch you cannot breathe deeply which means, there is less oxygen being taken into your lungs and therefore less oxygen available for your body and your brain to function effectively. This can result in breathlessness, fatigue, lack of energy and feeling tired all the time. Slouching and slumping puts the body out of alignment which may result in headaches and backache. It is now widely acknowledged that slouching can affect blood pressure. Slouching not only affects your physical health but it also makes you feel 'low' and 'down' whereas standing up straight makes you feel 'upbeat' and 'high'.

It's quite easy to adopt good posture: just loosen your arms and shoulders and imagine you are holding a £20.00 note between your shoulder blades. Try to get into the habit of doing this as often as you can so that good posture becomes the norm.

The second step is to breathe properly, about 90% of our energy is created by oxygen which regulates nearly all of the body's actions. It is recognised that cancer cells don't survive in oxygen so breathing effectively is extremely important in preventing it. Many of us over-breathe which has physical implications. Over-breathing is when we breathe more rapidly and shallowly. This means that the chest does not expand as much as it could and most of the air does not reach the bottom of the lung. This results in 'chest breathing' commonly known as 'hyperventilation'. You can check if you are a chest breather by placing your right hand on your chest and your left hand on your abdomen. As you breathe, see which rises more. If your right hand rises more, you are a chest-breather, if your left hand rises more, you are an abdomen-breather. If you, like me, are one of the many chest breathers the good news is you can train the body (Tom again) to improve its breathing technique and with regular practice you will breathe from the abdomen most of the time even while asleep. There are many abdominal breathing techniques and those of you who meditate and/or practise Yoga will have learned how to do this. For those of you not familiar with breathing techniques here is a simple one that you can use:

Place one hand on your chest and the other on your abdomen. Take a deep breath in, ensuring that the hand on the abdomen rises higher than the one on your chest, and hold it for a count of not more than 7. Slowly exhale through your mouth for a count of 8. As all the air is released, gently contract your abdominal muscles to completely empty the air from your lungs. It is important to remember that we improve our respiration not by inhaling more air but by completely exhaling. Repeat for a total of 5 deep breaths and try to breathe at a rate of one breath every 10 seconds or 6 breaths per minute. If you practice this regularly abdominal breathing will become automatic, as it was immediately, we took our first few breaths after entering this world. If you want to see abdominal breathing in practice look at a baby and you will see its stomach going up and down as it breathes. We all started life breathing properly but we can get out of the habit and, as we are not aware of it consciously, dysfunctional breathing becomes the norm. Breathing properly is one of the most beneficial things that can be done for both short- and long-term physical and mental health.

The third step is to make sure you are hydrated, and this means drinking plenty of water. Most people live in a constant state of dehydration simply because they do not drink enough water. There are so many negative effects of dehydration, some more critical than others. Primarily it can affect our kidneys as they are not able to remove the toxins from our body effectively because they don't have enough 'fluid' to flush our systems in the way they are meant. Stomach pain or heartburn, aching joints and muscles, headaches or migraines may be due to lack of water. Often, it's toxins in our body that cause these problems. Irritability or depression can also be a symptom of dehydration as well as dry skin, constipation, and even high blood pressure. Getting enough water is vital as it helps our circulation and our blood to transport nutrients and oxygen throughout the body. Drinking water also helps with fatigue, so next time you are feeling tired in the daytime or get the 'mid-afternoon slump' try drinking a glass of clean water – see if you notice the difference. Surprisingly, water retention can be eliminated by drinking more water. Keeping your body 'clean' and well flushed will pay dividends once you get into the habit, and you will soon realize that water goes well beyond simply quenching our thirst.

And there we have it! Three easy steps that can be done in less than five minutes which will improve your health by 25%. What does a 25% increase in your wellbeing look like?

Inside your body:
Standing or sitting straight gives all your vital organs more room to do their jobs properly. It exercises your muscles by stretching them, we build muscle this way making us stronger and fitter.

Better breathing supplies more oxygen for the nutrients in our bodies to increase our energy levels; more oxygen in the blood to our brain – which is the biggest user of oxygen in our bodies – helps us to think more clearly and feel happier, more capable and more content.

Drinking the right amount of water clears out the toxins from our organs and life systems - this alone eliminates many of the causes of the common aches and pains we suffer from daily. Less poison in our bodies allows our cells to grow more naturally, stay healthier and helps our immune system to fight diseases.

Outside your body:
You will tone your muscles, hold your posture better, have healthier looking skin, look and feel more positive, do more of the things you want to do, look more alert and be readier to respond to the trials and tribulations of the life you want to lead.

It really is that simple to make effective healthy change in our lives. So why aren't we all doing it then?

Part of the answer is so simple it is unbelievable. We don't really believe such little things will make much difference. And there you have it. We simply, deep down, don't believe it. Rationally we do. Our conscious mind will accept what I am saying, but that stubborn and belligerent Tom knows better and chants away in our inner ear, "I can't see that working, I can't see that working, I can't see that working." But he will let you try. And if you get yourself to make a new habit out of these three steps, within a week or two you will feel and SEE the benefit, then Tom will be with you all the way. So, practise!   Take it one step at a time, make it simple, something that can be fitted easily into your busy and stressful lives.   The more you practise the more it becomes automatic, just like driving. The best analogy is riding a bike. Before our first bike ride our conscious and subconscious brains knew that it should be impossible to balance on two wheels and until we try it the likes of Tom won't believe it. But once we have mastered it, once we start moving and we don't fall off, away we go! Tom's convinced and won't stop you riding a bike ever again. When we practise these changes, we make it part of a routine and then it becomes a habit. Start slowly – don't do a marathon or Tom will be finding a sore backside to nag you about and don't set your expectations too high. For example, you might make a promise to yourself to do these things three times a day to start with.   You could tie it into mealtimes or any other times that suit you better. Repeat this routine daily until it feels automatic and then increase it bit by bit. An example would be every time I stand up, I am going to make sure I have the correct posture and that I am breathing into my abdomen. That's not hard, it doesn't take up much time, but it will result in you doing it often so that it will become automatic very quickly.   Keep reminding yourself that this is a step-by-step process and sometimes you will not feel like doing it. Don't beat yourself up (or Tom), just decide to do it again when you feel up to it, or when you next remember to do it. Slowly but surely means that you will stick with it, and it will be long lasting. Every step you take is moving you forward - just remember that. Congratulate yourself on how far you have come instead of beating yourself up because you didn't do what you had set out to do.

Now for 'the Long Fix':
If you want to do more, then make sure that you are eating healthy food most of the time.   There are many options out there and I will give you details of these later in the book.   The choice is then yours.   However, if

like me, you like to keep things simple you might like to know that even though there are many different types of diet, the main things are the same. Put simply, you need to eat a balance of protein. i.e., chicken, fish, oily fish, red meat occasionally, beans, pulses, nuts and seeds. If you are vegetarian or vegan replace meat and fish with healthy natural substitutes like beans and pulses. Eat plenty of fresh fruit and vegetables.   Include good fats such as olive oil, coconut oil and butter but avoid bad hydrogenated fats such as margarine.   Avoid processed foods which contain chemicals, preservatives and added sugar.   Cut down on sugar, better still cut it out completely.   Wherever possible choose organic, not just for the taste but to avoid pesticides, chemicals and anti-biotics. Again, it's quite simple and although most of us know this we don't do it. Why?   For the same reasons we don't do what we need to do to stay healthy.

In the meantime, keep it simple and try to stick to these basics; even if you change just one thing you are moving forward on your journey to better health.   If you are reasonably healthy and your immune system is not compromised, then I believe in the 80/20 rule.   Eat healthily 80% of the time and then have some of the things that you enjoy that are not on the healthy list 20% of the time.   Oh, and by the way, alcohol is full of sugar so try to limit that to 20% of the time.   If you are an alcoholic and you are trying to stop drinking you need to cut out all sugar as well as alcohol in order to have the best chance of success because sugar can be as addictive as alcohol.

Now we look at exercise and all the evidence suggests it is as important, if not more important, than eating a healthy diet. When we talk about exercise we think of things like jogging, going to the gym working out, sports, etc. which fill many of us, me included, full of dread.   I hate all of that!   In the past I have paid for numerous gym memberships, and I've forced myself to go, but after a while I stop going. It may interest you to know that to be healthy you don't have to do any of those things, all you need to do is move.   Movement is exercise and walking is one of the best forms of exercise you can possibly do. Just getting out in the fresh air for 20-30 minutes is very good for you and it will provide you with vitamin D which is very important for health. It fights infections including colds, flu and viruses, it's important for reducing hypertension and the risk of heart disease, heart attack and stroke; it is also an immune modulator which makes it important in the prevention of autoimmune disease. It is estimated that over half of our society is deficient in vitamin D and although there are signs - such as having low mood, gut problems, excessive head sweating and aching bones - the only real way to tell is to have a blood test. If this shows a deficiency, it can be rectified with supplements which your doctor can prescribe.

I know that some of you who are reading this book may not be able to walk far - you may be in a wheelchair or even bed bound and so feel that you cannot exercise. But if you can't move your legs, then move your hands and arms, and if you are sitting most of the time stand up frequently. Do what you can do, however little, as that is a step in the right direction.

It is only recently that exercise has been put on a par with good diet. As many of us do sedentary jobs it is important that we get up and move frequently. It is possible nowadays to have a desk you stand at, and you can walk while you are working- almost like a treadmill. I recently saw a television program where children who were badly behaved in class were given one of those foot cycles which they had under the desk so they could cycle whilst learning. This produced surprising results and not only did their attention and behaviour improve but they lost weight too. These foot cycles cost very little, about £20, and anyone can use them. This may be the answer if you can't afford a standing desk or if you are immobile. There are details in the resources section where you can obtain this type of equipment.

From Frederic Patenaude's book entitled, "Our bodies are designed for movement".
This is an exact quote from his book:

"In a 24-hour day, humans are meant to move for roughly half the time. We don't think about it, but the body is very different when we sit.

As soon as you've been sitting down for a few minutes, the body starts to go into hibernation mode.
Calories burned drop to 1 calorie per minute (that's low!)
The enzymes that move bad cholesterol slow down.
The muscles in your lower body are literally turned off.
After two hours of sitting, good cholesterol drops by 20%
After a day of sitting, insulin sensitivity decreases by 24%
After two weeks of sitting for more than six hours a day, you increase your triglycerides, LDL cholesterol, and reduce insulin sensitivity by 40%
After one month of sitting for more than six hours a day, your muscles start to atrophy
After one year of sitting for more than six hours a day, you lose one percent of your bone mass
Sitting more than 6 hours a day makes you 40% more likely to die within 15 years than someone sitting 3 hours or less. That's EVEN if you exercise.
Sitting kills us.

What can we do?
Rethink your life.

I (Frederic Patenaude) chose to install a treadmill desk to work at home. This is not as quirky as it might sound. I have a desk that I can work at standing up. Where I stand is a treadmill, very like the one you would use in a gym. Whilst I am working at my desk - doing emails, making craft cards, sewing or whatever else I have planned to do that day – I set the treadmill at an easy walking pace. I don't wear a Fitbit, but I bet I easily exceed 10,000 steps every day I am at my desk.

You could decide to live in a city where you can walk everywhere and not have to drive much. You could get a dog and let Rover get you out and about.

Everyone can figure out what they can do to sit less and move more.

This isn't all or nothing, and every step in the right direction helps.

The book "Get Up! Why Your Chair is Killing You and What You Can Do About It" is a great place to get started. It's written by James Levine, the director of the Mayo clinic who started the treadmill desk trend.

Another good book is, "Sit less: The Office Fitness Book" by Larry Swanson, which goes into more practical details."

What else can we do?

An article by Christiane Northrup MD, based in the USA, talks about the huge debate on whether or not salt is good for your body. Despite the fact that it has been used to clean and heal wounds and sores and as a gargle to soothe sore throats the debate goes on as to whether it is good for the rest of your body. She says that the Food and Drug Administration (FDA) warns Americans to consume less than 2,300mg of sodium, also labelled as salt, per day; less than your kidneys can filter in five minutes! Other organisations recommend even less. But sodium is an essential nutrient that your body depends on and like any essential nutrient getting the right amount is important for maintaining good health. People are confused about salt, and she says that one of the reasons for this is that when it comes to dietary salt many people, doctors included, use the word salt and sodium interchangeably. However, they are not the same. Sodium is a mineral found in salt. Salt is a naturally occurring compound comprising of sodium and chloride. Then there is table salt, which is created from natural salt but then is refined, through a process of heating it to 1,200 degrees Fahrenheit, which destroys most of its beneficial compounds. To use the words sodium and salt as the same thing is not accurate. But, to confuse table salt with natural salt is where you get into real problems, as with any refined foods. Another area of confusion is the theory of why salt is bad for you. The theory stating that sodium (and therefore salt) causes high blood pressure stems from the myth that when you eat salt, you get thirsty and drink more water. Your body holds on to the extra water in order to dilute the saltiness in your blood. This results in increased blood volume, which the theory suggests leads to high blood pressure. Therefore, the theory states, a low sodium diet reduces blood pressure - although this theory has never been scientifically supported. Some studies actually show that salt helps your body conserve water and makes you less thirsty. Additional studies show that the connection between salt and high blood pressure is more complicated or even non-existent. The Framingham Offspring Study – an offshoot of the Framingham Heart Study - found that participants who ate a low sodium diet (under 2,500 milligrams of sodium per day) had higher blood pressure than those who consumed higher quantities. And more recent studies show that there really is no link between salt intake, high blood pressure, and risk of heart disease. She goes on to say that despite the fact that you will probably continue to hear messages that sodium is bad for you, your body cannot function without enough sodium and the best way to get enough is through dietary salt. She also refers to many studies that show the adverse effects of too little salt. Some of these adverse effects include insulin resistance and an increased risk of death in patients from heart failure, plus an increased risk of death for both type 1 diabetics and type 2 diabetics. Low-sodium or low-salt diets are also associated with elevated LDL cholesterol and triglycerides and low blood pressure (hyponatremia) which can be particularly concerning for certain populations such as athletes and the elderly. And these effects aren't just the result of purposeful salt restriction. Low-carbohydrate diets, such as Paleo and Keto and certain medications can cause sodium loss. Symptoms of sodium deficiency from salt restriction or poor salt absorption include dehydration, muscle cramps, headaches, weakness, irritability, and even cognitive decline. In addition, when you restrict salt, your body eventually will start to increase insulin to help your kidneys retain more sodium. Over time this can lead to chronically high insulin levels, a craving for sugar and refined carbohydrates, a cycle of weight gain, insulin resistance, and even diabetes.

In the next part of her article Dr Northrop goes on to talk about how much salt we need and where do we get it from. According to the American Heart Association (AHA) the minimum physiological requirement of sodium simply to sustain life is 500mg per day. However, in The Salt Fix, author James Dinicolantonio, PharmD, a cardiovascular research scientist at Saint Luke's Mid-America Heart Institute in St Louis, says scientists have found that when peoples' consumption of sodium is unrestricted, they typically consume between 3,000 to 4,000 milligrams per day. This amount holds true for people across all populations, in all hemispheres and climates, and across a range of cultures and social backgrounds. In other words, all humans gravitate towards the same sodium intake range every day. That's because this amount of sodium is optimal and is driven by the hypothalamus, the part of the reptilian brain that keeps your body in homeostasis (physiological equilibrium).

That said whether you need to increase your healthy intake of salt depends on many factors, including your diet and lifestyle. For example, if you eat a whole food diet, you may benefit from adding more healthy salt to your diet because unprocessed, all-natural foods are low in sodium. In addition, athletes, people who sweat a lot, people who take diuretics and other medications that cause sodium loss, and people recovering from adrenal fatigue can benefit from added natural salt. However, sodium is present in high amounts in processed foods where it is often used as a preservative or flavour enhancer - monosodium glutamate (MSG) and "natural flavourings". Even foods that don't taste salty can have high amounts of sodium, including breakfast cereals, and bread. So, if you are eating a lot of refined foods, you are probably already getting more than 4,000mg of sodium per day.

Adding natural salt to your diet is one of the easiest ways to ensure you get enough sodium and other essential minerals, especially if you are active. The most common natural salts are sea salt, Himalayan salt, and Celtic salt. Each has a unique flavour and mineral composition. For example, sea salt often contains high levels of trace minerals, including potassium, iron, and zinc. It also contains small amounts of natural iodine. Himalayan salt comes from the ancient seabeds of the Himalayan mountains. It is rich in iron, which gives it its pink colour, as well as 83 other essential trace elements, including magnesium, potassium and calcium. Celtic salt is hand-raked in Brittany, France, and is grey due to the clay and sand where it is harvested. It is a moist salt and is rich in many minerals. Other natural salts include black and red salt from Hawaii, and Fleur de Sel, a solar –evaporated sea salt typically used as a finishing salt.

Finally, if you suffer muscle cramps, have trouble sleeping, or crave salty foods, these are signs that you need more salt. Muscle cramps also indicate a need for more magnesium. If you want to increase your salt intake start by adding a little to your food. It's a great way to improve flavour and increase essential minerals. Salt also helps you to improve your digestive process by activating amylase (an enzyme that enables you to taste food) creating hydrochloric acid to support your stomach wall and stimulating intestinal and liver secretions to help break down food and aid digestion. Plus, salt adds a satiety factor, so it may encourage mindful eating and even help with weight management.

Track your salt intake to determine what level is optimal for you, try using an app such as My Fitness Pal. Track your intake when you enter your foods and then take notes regarding how you feel, your energy levels, sleep quality, and so on. After a few weeks you will notice what amount of salt you need to make you feel good. If you have been told to restrict sodium due to high blood pressure, be sure to track your blood pressure at home whilst increasing your salt intake. Make sure you speak with your health care provider before changing your diet or using any supplements and have your blood pressure checked during your visits.

It's important to maintain the correct balance of electrolytes (potassium and calcium as well as sodium) in order for your body to work optimally. To offset any potential imbalance whilst increasing salt, be sure to eat foods rich in potassium, including bananas, spinach, sweet potatoes, edame, cantaloupe and lentils. As with any new protocol listen to your body. Start by allowing your salt cravings to dictate how much salt you consume and in what form and then be sure to track how you feel.

*   *   *

"Finding yourself" is not really how it works. You aren't a five-pound note in last winter's coat pocket. You are not lost. Your true self is right there, buried under cultural conditioning, other people's opinions and inaccurate conclusions you drew as a kid that became your beliefs about who you are." "Finding yourself" is actually returning to yourself. An unlearning, an excavation, a remembering who you were before the world got its hands on you

Emily McDowell

Chapter 8

Finding Yourself – Onion Therapy

Onion Therapy is a process of discovery that works on anything. It enables you to discover who you are so that then, and only then, can you start to rebuild a 'better' happier, and contented you by learning to be at one with yourself.

There are 4 steps:

Step 1
Define and accept where you are now making a life balance wheel to give ideas.
For information on the Life Balance Wheel go to the website: www.oniontherapy.co.uk

Step 2
PEEL: Identify extremes in your life, physical and emotional, positive and negative i.e., extreme feelings of anger, anxiety, depression, frustration, sadness, not feeling good enough, lacking confidence, loneliness addictions etc., cancer and/or any physical illnesses that affect or impact your life.

Step 3
REVEAL: Find and understand the root cause of these extremes, believe that you can do something about it and create the desire to change.

Step 4
HEAL: Identify a bespoke strategy of change that suits both you and your lifestyle that you can implement and maintain.

Peel, reveal and heal. That is Onion Therapy in a nutshell.

PEEL:
Just what I did, but it took me a long time and an even longer time to heal the hurt and get back to where I needed to be. But I hope I can help you to get there and back much faster.

Look at yourself objectively right now and accept that is how you are. If you have a drink problem, a weight problem or you are addicted to drugs, shopping, gambling or anything else, this is the reality. If you are angry, lazy, have a health problem, be it physical, mental or emotional you need to have the courage to acknowledge and accept it. Not easy, because you have built layers to hide your faults from the outside world and perhaps layers to hide it from yourself too, so you are in denial. You might be doing okay, and you've been successful, as I was - but eventually you'll need to do something about it. That pinpoint moment in time for me was probably when I had fallen so far down that I could think of nothing else but to call The Samaritans. That was when my problems got so bad, and the battle inside myself to hide secrets became too fierce, that they manifested themselves in physical and emotional problems: severe psoriasis, binge comfort eating, physical breakdown and depression. You may have to reach your lowest ebb before you can admit you have a problem.

But, with Onion Therapy, it doesn't have to take so long or become so critical. I know, with practice, we can nip things in the bud. Are there facets of yourself that you don't understand? That maybe prompt a response from your inner voice that says, "I wish I didn't do that"? Anything that you feel is incongruent with your life can be explored and, in many cases, fixed.

In our modern society, when it comes to matters of health, we have come to put total faith in our medical profession. We have given control of much of our health and wellbeing to others; or, more often than not, we give control to a packet of pills. And, what's worse, we believe that most times they fix the problem. Isn't this what the doctor does? You tell him your symptoms; he prescribes some medication and says come back in two weeks if it doesn't go away! It goes away and we think it was the pills that sorted it.

Most drugs get onto the market after rigorous testing. Some of those tests involve blind trials where placebos are given instead of the active medicine and the participants don't know whether they were given medicine or placebo. In a percentage of cases those participants on placebos also show the result which was intended from the medicine.

Increasingly, we are all becoming aware of our bodies ability to cure itself. Most of us will have experienced a fear of 'coming down with something' to blight an important day – going on holiday, a wedding, an award ceremony or whatever, only to find that niggly little cough or sniffle has disappeared by the big day. The more you think about it the more you will realise that all of us have immense ability to overcome many things in life by taking the onus, control and responsibility for our health and wellbeing away from others and putting it onto ourselves.

To do this we need information. I found things out and came to conclusions the hard way, but by reading this book you can take that first step: admit who you are and acknowledge the things that are affecting your health and your life. I will give you as much information as I can in the best way I know.

Before we move onto the next part on Onion Therapy, I would like to introduce you to some research that seems to confirm the link between positive outcome thinking and health, wellbeing and longevity.

In 2009 Elizabeth Blackburn and Carol Greider won the Nobel prize for Physiology in Medicine for their work with telomeres. These little things are found at the end of our chromosomes and protect the tips from destruction; rather like the tips at the end of shoelaces protect the shoelace from fraying. What they discovered was that as we age these telomeres wear out which in turn reduces the effectiveness of our immune system. Their findings argue that to lengthen our telomeres, or at least stop them shortening, we need to improve our lifestyle by managing chronic stress, exercising, eating better, having a positive outlook and getting enough sleep. A lot of these things are recommended already – so what is new?

People hadn't understood why, at the cellular level, the sort of things that are recommended to improve lifestyle can help to stave off disease. One reason is because they are helping you to maintain telomeres. Elizabeth and Carol's work integrated a lot of new studies that have been accumulating – genetics, epidemiology and social science – and further work has provided a new biological underpinning to the mind-body connection. Nobody had any idea that meditation and the like, which people can use to reduce stress and increase wellbeing, would be having their salutary and well-documented useful effects in part through telomeres. This work recognises how much control we can have. Small tweaks in how you approach stress, for example, can lead to long-term habits that make a fundamental difference.

If you'd like more information on Elizabeth Blackburn and Carole Greider's work, you'll find links in the Resources chapter at the end of this book.

Now that you have accepted who you are and where you are at in your life, we can go to the next step of Onion Therapy: Identify what you want to change in your life.

REVEAL:
At this point in the process a large degree of common sense is presumed. Onion Therapy is a discovery process, and I would expect that most of you reading this book are content with your lot sufficiently so that radical change is ruled out. Positive change will come from small steps and adjustments to the way you go through each day, with a view to forming good new habits to replace old, out of date, unhelpful ones. All change requires motivation, a redirection of energy or a realignment of impetus in order to achieve different outcomes. If the change you need to effect is radical, as in the case of dealing with a diagnosis of a cancer disease, the motivation to change will be easier - on the same continuum as the Fight or Flight response - because you'll be thinking along the lines of, "If I don't change some things, I might die but if I do change some things, I might survive!" There's nothing like staring your own demise in the face to focus your mind and make you change direction.

Once you have made up your mind what you want to change, you need to go back to the cause. The particular change you want to effect will dictate to whom you go for help - a therapist, a practitioner, a trusted friend, a relative or a self-help group.

We all grow up more or less accepting what we are and the way we react to everyday situations. You have read that I grew up with the notion I was not good enough and didn't deserve success (whatever success is). It's when we begin to see the world through another's eyes that we see ourselves in a different light. Of course, it depends upon who you ask; that's why it's valuable to get a view from a professional therapist, practitioner, counsellor or consultant. These people won't judge you and they'll be entirely objective about whatever issue you bring. Choose someone who belongs to a professional body which supports their specialism. Ask for a free consultation initially, which can be just a telephone call. If you take a look on the website Steve and I have created – www.oniontherapy.co.uk – we have listed many types of complementary therapies with a brief summary of what to expect from each. Of course, you are welcome to contact me for advice and my contact details are again via the website.

In my experience most people have an idea of what's wrong before they seek help. You may be new to the idea of asking for help with something you feel is trivial and not worth bothering over, but if there's a feeling within you that something isn't right, and if that feeling wasn't there you would feel more at peace and at one with yourself, I will tell you for sure, that your subconscious - your gut feeling - is very astute and, if it feels that something isn't right, then something prevails that can be discovered and set right. Often, it's really simple: a misunderstanding or a confusion and a change of viewpoint is all that's required. If it's something deeper, then finding out sooner rather than later could be critical.

Upon discovery of your issue and how that manifests itself with you now, go back in your mind, again with help if you need to, to when you can first recall having this feeling of ill-ease. To do this, find a quiet moment in a quiet place where you can be alone with yourself for a few minutes. It's best not to do this just before you go to bed. Mornings are good. Ask your inner self to help, then run back in your mind as best you can to when you first had this feeling. Be peaceful with your eyes closed while you ask the question. Don't try and force any answers. After a few minutes, get on with your day and forget about the issue. Sometime during the next day or so, some answers will present themselves. Sometimes it may take longer, but don't force it. When you are as sure as you can be about a start point for your issue, you are then ready to do something about it. Take these answers to your therapist, or whoever you have chosen to help you.

HEAL:

When you have found yourself at this point Onion Therapy has done its job for you. The healing is out there and will involve some degree of change. I am a bit reluctant to use the term everyday issues, but it serves here to differentiate from the bigger stuff - cancers and the like.

If you have what you can call an everyday issue, which you want to do something about and you have found the most likely start point as outlined above, you need to motivate your inner self, as well as your conscious and rational self, to work together to change you for the better. Being realistic and sensible, decide what you want as an outcome and check on the resources you are going to need to start, maintain and complete the change. Then decide on a timescale that fits in with your outcomes. Build into your plan what you are going to do when you've achieved your goal. Leave room for flexibility, there will be discoveries along the way that you cannot know at the start, so be prepared for change. My healing, once I had peeled back the layers and revealed the causes of my issues, is continuing still, although I prefer to look at it as if I have gone beyond healing and am in a never-ending phase of continual assessment and improvement where anything I choose is possible.

Good luck, but now read on because the most amazing stuff is to come!

*   *   *

"My teacher Jim Rohn taught me a simple principle: every day, stand guard at the door of your mind, and you alone decide what thoughts and beliefs you let into your life.   For they will shape whether you feel rich or poor, cursed or blessed."

Tony Robbins

Chapter 9

The Power of Your Mind

On ATV television back in the early 1960s on a Saturday afternoon, there was a lady astrologer who had a five-minute slot just before the early evening news called "Fun with the Stars". She always signed off with her catch phrase: "Think lucky and you'll be lucky!" It's a pretty good guess that Evadne Price practiced what she preached; she had a fantastic career as a magazine and newspaper columnist for more than six decades, published hundreds of books, wrote screenplays for films, was an international TV broadcaster and lived until she was ninety-six years old. Since Evadne's day, there have been countless works detailing the power of positive thinking.

In its simplest form, in the context of everyday life, having a positive outlook is preferable to having a negative one. The greatest discoveries and inventions of mankind were never found by some hapless, negative, Victor Meldrew-type character who never aimed to succeed at anything except getting two feet in his grave! Even the cells in our bodies, as discovered by the Nobel Prize winning Medical Physiologists Elizabeth Blackburn and Carol Greider in their work on telomeres, respond to a positive disposition and appear to slow down the ageing process.

This phenomenon is at the heart of this book. The mind-body connection. How positive and negative dispositions not only affect your mental health, but your physical health, too. The power of the mind can be harnessed to change your beliefs and to change negative thoughts into positive ones. This can change your health and your life! How do I know? Because I've done it!

You might say positive thinking doesn't work and it doesn't in isolation, especially if you're unrealistic in aiming for absolute impossibilities - man powered flight and swimming around the world being such follies. But changing the word "thinking" into "feeling" holds the key to unlocking infinite possibilities.

In his book "Mind to Matter" Dawson Church reveals the astonishing science of how your brain creates material reality. It provides groundbreaking new scientific evidence that our thoughts have a direct impact on the world around us and it shows how to harness this knowledge so that we can live a full and effective life. There are many practical examples and exercises that enable you to work on your own personal transformation as well as scientific evidence to back this up.

The forward to the book was written by Dr Joe Dispensa, who healed himself using the power of his mind. His story is quite remarkable. In 1986 he was on a bike taking part in a triathlon, when he was hit by a truck which broke 6 vertebrae in his spine. He needed radical surgery called the Harrington Rod surgery and the prognosis was that he would probably never walk again. He said that if it had been anybody else, he probably would have recommended surgery, but he decided that it wasn't for him. Because he believed that the power that made the body function could also heal the body, he checked out of the hospital to begin reconstructing his vertebrae in his mind piece by piece. For 6 weeks he agonised and couldn't get his mind to concentrate on what he wanted. It would take him about three hours of closing his eyes and visually reconstructing every single vertebra in his mind, then starting again every time he lost his concentration. By the end of 6 weeks, he could go through the entire process without losing his attention. Then something clicked – he describes it as being like hitting the perfect shot with a tennis racquet when you hit the sweet spot in the centre – and, at that exact moment, he says his mind connected. He started noticing significant changes in his body, his motor function started coming back and his body began the journey to recovery and to change dramatically. He was back on his feet in 10 weeks and back training again in 12 weeks. He made a deal with himself that if he were ever able to walk again, he would spend the rest of his life studying the mind-body/mind-over-matter connection and that is what he has done since 1986. He has written many books, worked with countless individuals and organisations and there are lots of videos on You Tube. It took focus, determination, persistence and a massive leap of positive belief for it to work. Us ordinary mortals struggle at the first negative thought - "This'll never work!" nags Tom. Our limiting beliefs are stubbornly and firmly programmed in and beliefs such as 'I'm not good enough' make it a self-fulfilling prophecy by not doing the things that we know will help us to improve our health and our life. I am an example of this. To succeed in sticking to the healing process of the mind you'll need to discover what's stopping you; the process we outline in Onion Therapy is an excellent first step. You could say, "If at first you don't succeed, find out what's stopping you and, when you have, try, try again!". And if you are able to keep practising and sticking to the process that you've chosen there's every reason it will work for you.

If you'd like more evidence there are many, many published tales available in print and online. Another book that I would recommend about the power of the mind is called "The Power of your Subconscious Mind" by Dr Joseph Murphy. 42 years ago, he cured a malignant sarcoma by using the healing power of the subconscious mind. He believes his subconscious mind created the who he is and continues to maintain and regulate his vital organs. He shows you the scientific way he tapped into the realm of infinite power which enabled him to get what he really wanted in life: the desire to live a happier, fuller and richer life. The book focuses on the power of prayer which he has experienced in his own life, and he has talked with and worked with many people who have experienced it too. He says it is not the thing believed in that brings an answer to a man's prayer - it is when the individual's subconscious mind responds to the mental picture or thought which is in the mind. He says the law of life is the law of belief and belief can be summed up briefly as a thought in your mind.

Further evidence is provided by C. Norman Shealy, MD, PHD. He introduces a term "Energy Medicine" and suggests that this could be the future of health. He has devoted his career to finding out everything about "energies" - physical, emotional, mental, spiritual, how we can activate them for health, and he tests the energies himself. He says, "We are empty creatures" in the physical sense, for all structures in us, physical/emotional/mental are a part of the spectrum of energies. He asks who we are, "We who are encased in a fabric of energies?" He explores further and asks if the Cosmos, which is also connected and bound together by energies, is part of this same phenomena. His questions, his discoveries and his organisation of knowledge make fascinating reading. A common thread is that great damage to the physical body ultimately comes from mental and emotional trauma. He says that individuals who survive infancy feeling emotionally abandoned or abused, wind up with lifelong health issues which may not be just psychological. This is because the endocrine system – the system in our bodies that regulates and controls the production and flow of hormones around our circulatory system - is particularly damaged by this as happens with any long-term stress of any kind. The pattern of lifelong excess, over-activity of the sympathetic nervous system, or the fight or flight mechanism can be set in early life by many psychological traumatic events. This type of stress leads to what is called 'armouring of the body'. That is muscle tension, which can lead in time to any disease, including cancer. He goes on to say that muscle tension leads to various abnormalities, slumping of the shoulders (sometimes scoliosis), curvature to the side (kyphosis) and curvature backward mostly in the thoracic area (increased lordosis or sway-back). These postural abnormalities become progressively worse throughout life and compromise many functions including both heart and lungs. I know this from my own experience and most doctors agree that stress is the cause of most illnesses.

I now want to introduce a study started in the mid 1990's to look at the correlation of emotional trauma in childhood and illness onset in adulthood. Called 'The ACES Study', it demonstrates that emotional trauma is one of the most under-exposed epidemics and one of the root causes of chronic illness. ACES stands for Adverse Childhood Experiences.

The researchers originally looked at 17,500 adults. It showed that those with a high incidence of ACES had an increased risk of 7 out of the top 10 causes of death and 67% of all adults in the study said they had had an adverse childhood event.

The researchers found 10 different types of ACES; they chose things they had seen in the research that were commonly understood as emotional trauma. Things like physical and emotional neglect, physical, sexual or emotional abuse, incarceration of a family member, parents separating or divorcing, mental illness in the family, substance abuse, alcoholism of a parent and so on. Out of the ten ACES they chose, the results showed if you had 6 of those you had a 20-year reduction in lifespan. Having just four gave you a 400% increased risk of things like depression, Alzheimer's or mental illness and 2 showed 100% increased risk of auto-immune diseases. It goes on: 8 ACES points to a three-fold increase in the risk of lung cancer and 3½ times the risk of heart disease. Moderate levels of ACES demonstrated a six-fold increased risk of illnesses like chronic fatigue syndrome, fibromyalgia. The conclusions lead to very interesting possibilities for us all.

Studies of this magnitude involving so many participants have to be considered as giving accurate findings and this one suggests that 9 out of 10 conditions start in the mind.
Emotional wounds need healing, just the same as physical wounds, otherwise they will continue to affect your health. We create layers to suppress our emotional wounds, which have been shown to weaken our immune system and also sap our energy. In order to become truly well we need to deal with these buried emotions.

It is vital for our emotional health that when we are babies, we attach properly to our caregivers – our parents. There has been some major research looking at mother and baby interactions and, out of 6,000 adults studied, half reported that they didn't bond properly with their mother, often playing out with similar poor father relations as well. This leads on to difficulty with self-regulation, anxiety, depression, difficulties with memory, concentration, focus and difficulty in relationships in adulthood as well. How we attach in our main relationships in adulthood is often defined by how we related and attached to our parents.

Attachment and developmental traumas are part of emotional abuse. The findings go even further, to propose that it is highly possible severe untreated childhood trauma can be passed down genetically from traumatised fathers, damaging their DNA and passing these mutations through their sperm onto their offspring. Experiments on traumatised mice showed damaged and mutated DNA passing down through seven generations.

When we start to release these traumatic emotions, we become transformed. Through the process of finding out how my past was affecting my health and lifestyle, limiting my options and making me unhappy and unfulfilled and then discovering treatments, therapies and processes, transformed my life completely. Deep emotional healing not only made me feel different but changed my outlook on my life and I became different. My focus has changed, my interests and passions have changed too, because I am no longer held back by the emotional effects of trauma and the belief that I am not good enough.

This is my Onion Therapy journey: I have peeled back all the layers right back to my beginning and then, step by step, come forward right up to the present day. I don't suggest you bare your soul to the world in a book like I have. We are all different, unique and you will find your own path to success that's right for you. It's taken me until I'm sixty-one years old to write this first book, mainly because I never felt good enough. I never felt good enough because my Mum died before I could get to know her; by the age of nine I already wasn't good enough. I then did some things that I carried with me far into adulthood that I thought were my fault. These cemented my belief even further that I was not worthy of achieving anything worthwhile. I believed relationships were out of bounds because I was hopeless at them, and everything pointed to it being my fault.

Who knows what I could have achieved if I had dealt with these issues when I was younger?

*   *   *

Don't dance so fast

Have you ever watched kids
On a merry-go-round?
Or listened to the rain
Slapping on the ground?
Ever followed a butterfly's
erratic flight?
Or gazed at the sun into the
fading night?
You better slow down.
Don't dance so fast.
Time is short.
The music won't last.

Do you run through each day
On the fly?
When you ask "How are
you?"
Do you hear the reply?
When the day is done
Do you lie in your bed
With the next hundred
chores
Running through your head?

*You'd better slow down
Don't dance so fast.
Time is short.
The music won't last.*

*Ever told your child,
We'll do it tomorrow.
And in your haste,
Not see his sorrow?
Ever lost touch,
Let a good friendship die
Cause you never had time
To call and say "Hi"?
You'd better slow down.
Don't dance so fast.
Time is short.
The music won't last.*

*When you run so fast to get
Somewhere
You miss half the fun of
getting there.
When you worry and hurry
through your day,
It is like an unopened gift ….
Thrown away.
Life is not a race.
Do take it slower
Hear the music Before the
Song is over.*

Author Unknown

Chapter 10

What If You Already Have Cancer?

When applied to cancer diseases, we cannot know when the start point might be or might have been, but in all cases, there has to have been one. You might now be asking, "Well then, what good is that if we cannot ever know?" I asked the very same question when I first explored this.

There have been thousands of studies and there will be yet thousands more before the human race comes up with a unified and definitive answer as to how to avoid or evade cancer. But what we have found and how we can apply changes to our lives based on those findings will lead to increasing our chances of dodging the disease and enable us to live a long and meaningful life. And, even if we do get a cancer, as I have seen first-hand with my work for The Loughborough Cancer Self Help Group, we can vastly increase our chances of beating it, or at least keeping it at bay and living longer with it, by making a few changes to the way we live and the way we think.

Cancer is often labelled as a lifestyle disease and there is a fair body of evidence to support this, and it does concur with the proliferation of cancer throughout the modern world. Ironically as life expectancies increase so do the instances of cancer; to be blunt, the longer we live the more likely it is we will get cancer. Is it then an ageing condition and therefore an inevitability if we live until we are old? As we get older our immune systems become less effective and we are more susceptible to defective cell growth which leads to malignant tumours rendering our vital organs less effective.

All of this is widely accepted, understood and, you could say, true.

If you already have cancer, then the first thing is - don't panic!! Easier said than done, I know!

After you have had the tests for cancer, you are given an appointment to discuss the results. Before you go write down all the questions that you want to ask. If you want a comprehensive list of questions, go to www.chrisbeatcancer.com and download his free guide '20 questions to ask your oncologist'. The guide is comprehensive and covers many things that you may not have thought of asking. If you go on your own, then ask if you can record the conversation on your phone so that you don't forget anything. However, if you can, take someone with you. I go with my friend to all of her appointments, and I take a notebook and write everything down. I also ask questions myself and if I am not sure what he means I will ask him for clarification. Having someone with you, especially if it is your partner, a family member or a close friend is also good from another perspective. It means that they can share your journey with you, it enables them to support you better and it means that you are not alone on your cancer journey. This may not be the right approach for everyone, some of you may prefer to go on your own, others may not have a choice but to go alone, and if this is the case, make sure you record the meeting or take a notebook and write everything down.

When you have all the information from that first meeting do not be railroaded into treatments that you haven't had a chance to think about and research. At this stage I recommend that you read "The Topic of Cancer" by Jessica Richards. Jessica Richards was diagnosed with cancer in 2007 and she decided to take a radical route to managing her own health. Years later she is fit and well and the book is not only a testament to her choices, but a commitment to helping others to manage their own illness: from diagnosis, through decisions about their health and wellbeing throughout the process to whatever methods of treatment they choose.

Think about the treatments that are right for you, even if they differ from what your oncologist wants you to have. Be honest with your oncologist, give him the reasons why you want to go down another route, ask him to respect your decision and ask if he will support you. You can always ask for a second opinion, but when you are stressed, in shock, and feel under pressure it is very difficult to do. That is why it's always best to have someone with you who can make sure you get what you want. Don't forget it is your life, your journey and everyone is different. What is right for one is not necessarily right for another and don't forget no one treatment fits all. It is important that you have control of your health with the support of the clinicians and not the other way around. If you don't have that support, then you need to change your clinician. If you choose a non-conventional, holistic approach to your cancer journey you may find that people will try to change your mind, but remember, that's because they don't have access to the information that you have. My aim, in writing this book, is to provide you with information to make an informed decision, and to make the decision that is right for you, whether it be conventional treatment, alternative or a combination of both.

If you decide to go against the 'norm' it is a big decision, and you need to have hope and believe that what you are doing is right. At this point I recommend that you read Kelly A. Turner's book "Radical Remission, Surviving Cancer against All the Odds". This is an excellent motivational book as she has researched remission from cancer and how we can shift the odds of remission in our favour. The book shows how it is possible to triumph over cancer, even in situations that seem hopeless. Every chapter includes dramatic stories of survivors' journeys back to wellness.

I also recommend that you have a look at the website of cancer survivor Chris Wark: www.chrisbeatcancer.com and read all the survivor stories. Not only will this give you motivation, something you need an abundance of, but it is proof that cancer is not a death sentence. Cancer is merely a wakeup call telling you things need to change.

Once you have decided what treatments are right for you, make a plan. Decide on what you are going to do and the changes you are going to make. Your objective is to take any pressure off your immune system so that it has the best chance of doing its job and killing off the cancer cells. As over 70% of your immune system is in your gut that means you need to look at your diet and make sure that your body is getting all the nutrients, vitamins and minerals that it needs.

Chris Wark's website is a good place to start when it comes to diet as he will give you details of what he did to heal his colon cancer. Professor Jane Plants book, "Your Life in your Hands" is the story of how her training and knowledge as a natural scientist enabled her to understand and eventually overcome her cancer. Her diet is different to Chris's, but the basics are the same. In her book, "The Plant Programme", together with fellow scientist Gill Tidey, she provides hundreds of tasty, easy to make and nutritious dairy-free meals for all occasions as well as tips on how to cope when dining away from home. Another good book is, "Do you want to know what we did to Beat Cancer?" This book, by her husband Robert Olifent, is the story of Sue Olifent's cancer recovery using natural principles and the diet and lifestyle changes she made.

So, diet is a priority. However, remember I said that if you are healthy, you can apply the 80% 20% rule? Well, if you have cancer you need to commit to 100% healthy eating if you are to give your immune system the very best chance of fighting off the cancer cells. Another thing that makes sense is that because digestion takes a lot of energy, making healthy vegetable juices, smoothies and soups is an excellent way of getting vitamins and minerals into your system without it having to do too much work. This has been known about for years – remember that excellent little book 'Chicken Soup for the Soul' playing on the old remedy of chicken soup given to a child who had a cold or fever?

There are many more diets that have been used successfully by people with cancer. For example, the Gerson diet, the Ketogenic diet or the Budwig diet to name but a few. If you haven't heard of them have a look on the internet to see if they make sense to you. The fundamentals are the same: eat only natural healthy and nutritional food, organic wherever possible. Cut out processed foods, cut out sugar which feeds cancer cells and in most cases dairy which contains growth hormones.

What about supplements? If your body is getting the right amount of fibre, vitamins and minerals from your diet then you don't need supplements. However, if you have cancer, your body may be severely depleted and may need some help. Even if you are well and eat a healthy diet there can be a problem due to the fact that over the years there has been a big depletion of minerals in soil. The soil report from the Earth Summit shows the following depletion during the past 75 to 85 years:

North America 85%
South America 76%
Asia 76%
Africa 74%
Europe 72%
Australia 55%.

There are various reasons for this: our diet has changed dramatically since the 1930s and 1940s. In addition, farming began to change from natural farming processes, developed over 1000's of years, to scientific farming processes. These patterns have run in parallel with lifestyle changes, disease pattern changes and food processing changes. One supplement, which doctors agree most of us are lacking in the UK, is vitamin D, so it is worth getting your doctor to check your vitamin D levels. And don't forget to make sure that the salt you use is natural sea salt so that it has iodine in it. There are a variety of other supplements that functional health doctors recommend for people who have cancer. Doctor Heather Paulson, a naturopathic doctor, has listed her top five as:

1 Vitamin D
2 Melatonin
3 Fish Oils
4 Sulphorphanes
5 Berry Extracts

If you want to read why, have a look on her website www.drpaulson.com. Notice she puts Vitamin D at the top of her list.

You may want to talk to a nutritionist too as they will make sure you have the right dose for your particular situation - but make sure that you talk to a registered one as anyone can set themselves up as a nutritionist or diet expert. Registration is voluntary and those who are registered are trained through the Institute of Optimal Nutrition and other formal routes. Nutritional therapists use treatments such as high dose vitamins, detox and food avoidance for which there is not a lot of scientific evidence. The main reason for that is because the pharmaceutical industry is not interested in doing research on things that are not going to make a profit. Nutritionists use commercial dietary supplements including mega doses of vitamins and minerals and commercial allergy testing. Under their voluntary register, nutritional therapists are allowed to sell supplements to their clients. They are also qualified to provide information about food and healthy eating. Nutritionists work in non-clinical settings such as in government, the food industry, research, teaching, sports and exercise industries, international work in developing countries, media and communications, animal nutrition and Non-Government Organisations (NGO's). There are some nutritionists employed within the NHS working alongside registered dieticians. The difference between nutritionists and dieticians is that dieticians are the only qualified health professionals to assess, diagnose and treat dietary and nutritional problems. Dieticians have to be regulated in law to work in the NHS, private practice, industry, education, research, sport, media, public relations, publishing, government and NGO's. They advise and influence food and health policies across the spectrum, from government to local communities and individuals. You will more often than not be given dietary advice by a dietician when you are diagnosed with cancer. Sometimes this advice will conflict with the advice given by a nutritionist and that is why I urge you to look at all the information and facts before deciding on what is right for you. Also, check the qualifications and background of anyone that you are going to be taking advice from, to satisfy yourself that they are appropriately qualified and regulated. Always discuss what you have decided to do with your GP and consultant. It is important to remember that this is your journey, and you need a consultant who is going to support you even if it is not something they would advise. If you do not get the support this can be difficult as you might find yourself conforming and agreeing to treatments that you really do not want. This is where a supportive friend or family member can help by being strong on your behalf, making sure you're in control and get what you want.

At the Cancer Self-Help Group in Loughborough, we pay for our members to see a qualified nutritionist, and this has always been the case since it started in 1983. Dr Patrick Kingsley who worked with our Cancer Group until he died, always recommended supplements to the members with cancer. In fact, our founding member Joyce Walton used supplements as part of her healing process, and she still uses them to this day. My business partner, Albert, was prescribed high doses of supplements: - Vitamin D, Liposomal vitamin C, Selenium, Alpha Lipoic Acid and high absorption CoQ10 by Patrick as part of Patrick's regime and Albert has been cancer free now for six years.

The doses vary from person to person as everyone is different. Other practitioners may recommend different or additional supplements but don't forget to get the support of your doctor if you are going to take them.

Once you've decided how you're going to change your diet and whether or not you are going to take supplements, the next thing to do is make sure that you deal with stress. Having cancer is stressful both physically and mentally, so you need to adopt techniques that will help to minimize it. And don't forget stress is the cause of over 90% of physical illnesses so it is very important to prioritise it. Reading the techniques described in "The Quick Fix" in Chapter 8 will help you to deal with the symptoms. But if you want to deal with the cause you will need to adopt some of the further suggestions in chapter "Finding Yourself".

It's a good idea to implement as many techniques and therapies as you can, to give your body the best chance of healing. Things like mindfulness, affirmations, meditation and complementary therapies; and take up a hobby which takes you out of your comfort zone, something that is relaxing and needs concentration, like painting and drawing, model making, knitting, crochet, etc.

Visualizations can make a massive difference. Remember Dr Joe

Dispensa who healed his broken back by visualizing his vertebra healing one by one? Joyce Walton who started our Cancer Group always used visualizations on her cancer journey and she still uses them to this day. She visualized her cancer cells being surrounded with love and becoming healthy again whereas another co-founder of the Loughborough group, Gill Hurd, used a more aggressive approach and visualized chickens pecking away at the cancer cells. Visualizations are easy and effective; they can be done at any time, and you can create your own to suit you.

Joining a Cancer Support Group has been shown to make a big difference to people's wellbeing. Socializing with people who have been there and done that will help you to overcome your fear. Access to information, that you might not otherwise have had, will help you to make informed choices and complementary therapies will help you to relax. There are many more benefits to joining a support group, but I appreciate they are not for everyone.

What else can you do?

This is a difficult one - be honest with your partner or carer about how you are feeling. Why? Keeping everything bottled up inside is more stressful than letting it out. I have seen this many a time at our group. The person with cancer doesn't want to admit to their partner that they're frightened because they're worried it will upset them. The partner doesn't want to tell the person who has cancer that they're frightened either for the same reason. And yet deep down they each know the other is frightened but they are just not saying it. It's going to be upsetting, but you're both upset anyway, so just be honest with each other, tell each other everything you are feeling, and you will feel much better. It will make things easier, too.

Let's take a step back now and consider what cancer actually is.

Cancer is the name given to a collection of related diseases. Cancer can start almost anywhere in the human body, which is made up of trillions of cells. In all types of cancer, some of the body's cells divide without stopping and spread into surrounding tissues. Normally, human cells grow and divide to form new cells as the body needs them. When cells grow old or become damaged, they die, and new cells take their place. When cancer develops, however, this orderly process breaks down. As cells become more and more abnormal, old or damaged cells survive when they should die, and new cells form when they are not needed. These extra cells can divide without stopping and may form growths called tumours. Many cancers form solid tumours, which are masses of tissue. Cancers of the blood, such as leukaemia, generally do not form solid tumours. Cancerous tumours are malignant, which means they can spread into, or invade, nearby tissues. In addition, as these tumours grow, some cancer cells can break off and travel to distant places in the body through the blood or the lymph system to form new tumours far from the original tumour. Cancer cells differ from normal cells in many ways that allow them to grow out of control and become invasive. One important difference is that cancer cells are less specialized than normal cells. That is, whereas normal cells mature into very distinct cell types with specific functions, cancer cells do not. This is one reason that, unlike normal cells, cancer cells continue to divide without stopping. In addition, cancer cells are able to ignore signals that normally tell cells to stop dividing or that begin a process known as programmed cell death, or apoptosis, which the body uses to get rid of unneeded cells. Cancer cells may be able to influence the normal cells, molecules and blood vessels that surround and feed a tumour—an area known as the microenvironment. Cancer cells are also often able to evade the immune system, a network of organs, tissues, and specialized cells that protects the body from infections and other conditions. Although the immune system normally removes damaged or abnormal cells from the body, some cancer cells are able to "hide" from the immune system. There are more than 100 types of cancer. Types of cancer are usually named from the organs or tissues where the cancers form. For example, lung cancer starts in cells of the lung, and brain cancer starts in cells of the brain.

What are the causes? It is a very complex and different combination of things for each individual, but if you Google the question, as I did, these are some of the things you will find: Cancer starts with gene mutations and most mutations happen after you're born and aren't inherited (this ties in with what Bruce Lipton proved scientifically, that only about 1% of cancers can be attributed to genes). The rest are due to environmental factors such as age, smoking, radiation, viruses, cancer-causing chemicals (carcinogens), hormones, inflammation, diet, alcohol, lack of exercise and immunosuppression. Let's examine these one at a time and see what we can do to lessen the risk, not only of getting cancer but other diseases too.

There are several major factors that can cause cancer.

Firstly: AGE – well we can't do much about that except by taking note of the how telomeres are affected by lifestyle conditions, a positive or negative attitude and by taking care of ourselves to minimise the risk of getting ill so we can look forward to a long, happy and healthy life. Age should not mean that we become ill and lose our capacity to enjoy life - there are many examples of people in their eighties, nineties and even their hundreds who still have all their faculties and are enjoying a fit and active life. However, we are all going to die at some stage as even if we take good care of ourselves our bodies are going to wear out, so living a fit and active life for as long as we can is the best that we can do.

Secondly: SMOKING - now here is something we can change – or can we? Smoking is an addiction, and most smokers say they would like to give up, but they can't – and I can relate to that because I was one of them. Because it is partly an addiction and people believe that it is hard to give up it is hard. But if you change that belief, it becomes easier. Some people believe that they will put on weight if they stop and for others it is the fear of losing their identity as 'a smoker' and no longer fitting in. For many people, as it was with me, smoking is a way of numbing the brain and helping to keep stress and uncomfortable emotions at bay. Many people attempt to give up and are unsuccessful, so they beat themselves up for failing. After several attempts and several failures this just reiterates the belief that it is difficult. That was me, but I did give up. At the time, I didn't know anything about these hidden beliefs, so how did I do it? After several attempts at going 'cold turkey' setting a start date and giving away all my cigarettes the evening before, I realised that method was not working. So, I decided to adopt a different strategy, a different mind-set: I didn't get rid of my cigarettes, I kept them and said to myself, "Today I am going to see how long I can go without having a cigarette." As a heavy smoker I was smoking up to 40 a day and every day began with a cigarette. But on this particular day I opened the pack and asked myself if I really needed it now or could I wait a while. Although I had the craving, I decided I could wait for half an hour; if the craving were too bad, I had my cigarettes with me and I could have one whenever I wanted. Having got past the first half hour I continued with this strategy until, before I realised it, I'd got through a whole day without having a cigarette. I started day two on a high and told myself that if I could go without for one day then I could do the same for two which I did and so on and so on. This continued for a week, then a month and I was on a roll. By this time the cravings had reduced, and it was just a matter of breaking the habits I had got used to as a smoker. In my day nearly everyone smoked, which presented me with another obstacle to overcome. People would offer me a cigarette and I was so used to taking one it had become a habit. The mistake I made was to say, 'No, thank you, I've given up.' Instead of respecting that, I found people tried to convince me to have one, saying one won't hurt, etc. Even friends who didn't normally offer me a cigarette when I was 'a smoker' couldn't wait to offer me one when I wasn't. So, a word of advice, if you're going to give up smoking don't tell anyone. Just refuse the cigarette they offer saying you've just had one or you're not feeling well – anything except that you're giving up! So that's how I did it; I used trickery to get through.

Thirdly: RADIATION – What is radiation? In simple terms it is the emission or transmission of energy in the form of waves or particles through space or through material medium. This includes electromagnetic radiation such as radio waves, visible light and x-rays, particle radiation such as a, b and neutron radiation. e.g., ultraviolet light from the sun, heat from a stove burner, visible light from a candle, x-rays from an x-ray machine, alpha particles emitted from the radioactive decay of uranium, sound waves from your stereo, microwaves from microwave ovens, electromagnetic radiation from your cell phone, microwave radiation from your Wi-Fi router, radio waves, laser beams, ultraviolet light from black light - UVA lamps, radio waves and laser beams.

To reduce the risk there are a lot of things we can do: Turn our Wi-Fi router off when we are not using it. When using cell phones, use headsets rather than hold the phone to your ear. Do not put cell phones in pockets next to your skin, keep them in handbags or other receptacles. Do not use laptops on your lap, place them on a worktop instead. Keep your bedroom free of gadgets that emit radiation: that's anything from stereos, clock radios, tablets, alarms to TVs. Do not wear gadgets like fitness trackers that measure your activity or phone watches. Do not overexpose yourself to ultraviolet light by using tanning machines. Limit your exposure to the sun's rays, especially when they are at their strongest. Do not have smart meters installed in your house to measure power usage.

Those are just a few things you can do. I'm not saying don't do any of them at all, but now you know that they are harmful and can contribute to illnesses such as cancer, you can make informed choices. There are also products you can get that will help to reduce the effect – such as little discs you can put on your computers and cell phones and things you can plug in to sockets next to your Wi-Fi router. I don't know how effective they are, but evidence suggests it can reduce the effect by about 40%. Not many people know what is and what isn't radiation, and some things may come as a surprise to you, as they did to me. Radiation does damage health. If you have to have x-rays or radio therapy, you are told about the damage it can do. Many people who've had cancer and have had radio therapy are now suffering the consequences as it has damaged other organs. Joyce Walton who started the Cancer Self-help Group in Loughborough has damaged lungs as a result of her radio therapy. However, she made the choice with the knowledge that she had at the time. She weighed up the pros and cons and decided she could live with the damage if it saved her life. Radio therapy has improved, and they are now able to target it more effectively which minimises the damage.

In at number four: VIRUSES. The main ones associated with human cancers are HPV (human papilloma virus), hepatitis B and hepatitis C virus, Epstein-Barr virus, human T-lymphotropic virus, Kaposi's sarcoma-associated herpes virus (KSHV) and Merkle cell polyomavirus.

Number five on our list of cancer causes are: CANCER CAUSING CHEMICALS – CARCINOGENS.

Well, this is a minefield. There are 111 chemicals known to cause cancer. However, those are only the ones that are known. To keep it simple I'd say that all chemicals are a risk, because anything we introduce into our bodies that the immune system does not recognise will cause a problem. Chemicals are not something that the immune system is set up to deal with and so it makes sense to avoid them wherever possible. Not easy I'm afraid because we are surrounded by them. Let's start with processed foods, which are on the known list of cancer-causing carcinogens and are one of the biggest culprits. So why are processed foods such a problem? Because the immune system doesn't recognise chemicals. The immune system recognises two things: infections and viruses and it knows what it needs to do to deal with them. It doesn't know what to do with chemicals; it does its best to eliminate them from the body but often it doesn't succeed, or in trying to eliminate them they get sent to the detoxifying organs such as the liver where they get stuck. Your immune system is comprised of the following: thymus and bone marrow, lymphatic tissues such as spleen, tonsils, lymph vessels, lymph nodes, adenoids, skin, liver and digestive tract. Between 70% and 80% of your immune system is in your digestive tract – your gut. So, what we put in there clearly has an enormous effect on our wellbeing. Our intestines are protected from our blood stream and our main life force system and are therefore actually "outside" your body. When the integrity of the gut is compromised, it can lead to "leaky gut" which means that the body is no longer protected against "invaders" like undigested food, gluten and bacteria that have passed through the gut lining. A leaky gut gives rise to food intolerances which can eventually lead to autoimmune conditions and other problems such as Chrohn's disease, Multiple Sclerosis, Eczema, Psoriasis, Arthritis, Migraine headaches and depression.

Research has revealed that a diet rich in whole, unprocessed foods will encourage the growth of good bacteria in the gut, boosting the action of the immune cells are certain strains of gut flora that prevent pathogens from being absorbed. It is so important to have colonies of "good bacteria" in the gut to establish a strong immune system. In fact, without the right balance of gut flora your body cannot maintain good health. There are other specific steps which you can take - read Shulzhenko's report in 'Clinical Reviews in Allergy and Immunology' - again, I have included links at the end of the book. She emphasises that our intestines contain more immune cells than the entire rest of our bodies and that the human gut plays a huge role in our immune function. According to her emerging theory, disease is a disruption in the "crosstalk" between the microbe in the human gut and other cells involved in the immune system and metabolic processes. She adds that things in modern lifestyles - diet and overuse of anti-biotics - are causing an increasing disruption of the gut microbes that stimulate the immune system. This causes inflammation linked to most of the diseases that kill people in the developed world today and may begin with disruption to our gut microbe balance.

Pre and probiotics are powerful immunity boosters. Probiotics are cultures of beneficial bacteria which include Lactobacillus acidophilus and Bifidobacterium bifidum. Prebiotics feed the good bacteria making sure that they can grow and flourish. Eating Probiotics in the form of fermented foods such as live yoghurt, sauerkraut, pickles, kefir, tempeh, kimchi, miso and kombucha, together with increasing fibre intake, increasing Omega- 3 fatty acids and decreasing the levels of Omega- 6 in the diet, getting enough sleep, getting regular exercise and lowering stress levels will all help to boost your immune system. Things that will weaken the immune system are stress, use of antibiotics, diarrhoea, deficient diets and environmental pollutions; a weak immune system can be caused by infections such as HIV/Aids, TB, cancer and ageing, and we need to be more proactive with these in most cases. There are supplements that you can take to lessen the effect, but it is always recommended you see a nutritionist rather than self-prescribing. This will save you time and money and will ensure that the treatment is unique to you. It is always a good idea to take prebiotics and probiotics when having anti biotics - just a short course can upset your gut bacteria for about 18months. If you decide to take these, I do advise that you get advice from a nutritionist first.

If we take care of our gut and protect it wherever possible from chemicals, we will make huge steps towards a fully functional immune system. Changing just some of the things referred to is a positive step forward.

Chemicals are everywhere and, in some instances, there is very little you can do. Not only is our outdoor environment polluted but our indoor environment - we are exposed to chemicals day and night. Air pollution causes damage to crops, animals, forests and reservoirs. It also contributes to the depletion of the ozone layer which protects the earth from the suns UV rays; it causes haze and contributes to global climate change. Most of the air pollution we cause results from burning fossil fuels such as coal, oil, natural gas and gasoline to produce electricity and power our vehicles. The solution to pollution is in everyone's hands and here are just a couple of things that you can do that will make a massive difference. Recycle everything you can and dispose of trash properly. What about indoor pollution? It might surprise and shock you to know that the average home today contains 62 toxic chemicals. Since World War II more than 72,000 chemicals have been produced and yet only 2% of synthetic chemicals have been tested for toxicity. Unbelievable! Some of the common household items that put your health at risk: Air fresheners, upholstery cleaners, oven cleaners, soap, washing up liquid, bleach, furniture polish, stain remover, toilet bowl cleaner, flame retardants in couches, mattresses and carpets, aerosols and sprays, paint, dry cleaning chemicals, perfume, cosmetics and personal care products. Here is something else that may shock you, out of 13,000 chemicals used in cosmetics only 10% have been tested for safety. According to statistics in the USA the average woman uses 12 personal care products each day which contain 168 different chemicals. The average woman uses 5lbs of cosmetics per year that is nearly half a stone of chemicals being absorbed by our immune system – through the skin. Unlike the gut, the skin is an excellent drug delivery system with no protection. Everything you put onto your skin is absorbed into your body. At least the microbiome (gut bacteria) in your gut helps to protect you from some of the toxins you ingest by filtering them.

As a quick guide I have put together a list of things to avoid and why:
PARABENS – a study in 2012 found parabens from anti-perspirants and cosmetics appear to increase the risk of breast cancer.

BHA and BHT used as preservatives in make-up and moisturisers are suspected endocrine disrupters.
Synthetic colours derived from coal tar or petroleum sources are suspected carcinogens and are linked to ADHD in children.

Fragrances fall into the large category of chemicals that are protected proprietary information.   Would you believe that manufacturers do not have to release the concoctions they use to produce the scents? And this applies to perfumes, shampoos and body washes!

TRICLOSAN - is an antibacterial ingredient found in soaps and other products and has been linked to allergies, endocrine disruption, weight gain and inflammatory responses.

FORMALDEHYDE – this is banned as it is a known carcinogen, but manufacturers use other chemicals that act as preservatives and release formaldehyde.   Chemicals such as quaternuim-15, diazolidinyl urea, methenamine and hydantoin are used in a variety of cosmetics and slowly release formaldehyde as they age.

SODIUM LAURYL SULFATE and SODIUM LAURETH SULFATE – are surfactants found in more than 90% of cleaning products and personal care.   They are used to make the product foam.   They are known to irritate the eyes, skin and lungs and may interact with other chemicals to form nitrosamines a known carcinogen.

TOULENE – made from petroleum or coal tar is found in most synthetic fragrances and polish.   Chronic exposure is linked to anaemia, lowered blood cell count, liver or kidney damage and may affect a developing foetus.

PROPYLENE – this small organic alcohol is used as a skin conditioning agent and is found in moisturisers, sunscreen, conditioners, shampoos and hair spray. It has been added to medications to allow your body to absorb chemicals more quickly and to electronic cigarettes. Smokers take note!   It is a skin irritant, toxic to your liver and kidneys and may produce neurological symptoms.
This is just the tip of the iceberg.

I find it incredible that manufacturers are able to use all of these chemicals, most of which have not been tested.   Even tested chemicals in my opinion should be banned - all chemicals cause our immune system a problem.   It would be very difficult to cut them out completely, but you can cut down. Try to avoid chemicals and use natural products wherever possible. There are more and more of these coming onto the market but be careful.   Products labelled "all natural" may still contain harmful chemicals so always check the list of ingredients to make sure.

We can all contribute to stopping pollution by using environmentally safe products, recycling everything we can, disposing of rubbish properly, refraining from flushing contaminated liquids, pills, drugs or medications down the toilet. Also, by ensuring minimal use of bleach, detergents, herbicides, pesticides and fertilisers.   When we think about all of this, and the polluted air we are breathing in, is it any wonder that over 5.5 million people in the UK are currently suffering from asthma?   Living by a road increases the risk. However, if you live by a road there are things you can do: Plant trees and hedges in front of the house to clean the air. Trees absorb odours and pollutant gasses (nitrogen oxides, ammonia, sulphur dioxide and ozone) and filter particulates out of the air by trapping them on their leaves and bark. However, research suggests that hedges are often better at soaking up air pollution among tall buildings. Councils plant trees in towns and cities to reduce pollution and the best trees are elms, common ash, wild linden, Norway maple, Turkey Oak, Ginkgo Biloba or broad –leaved linden. Not everyone will be able to plant trees and hedges so do what you can - plant trees in pots and if you can't do any of that, tackle pollution inside with plants. Plants are also effective in removing pollutants like formaldehyde, benzene and carbon monoxide from the air. They are all effective but here are some examples, Areca Palm, Lady Palm, Dwarf Date Palm, Bamboo Palm, Philodendrons, spider plants, rubber plants, Boston fern, Peace Lily and Ivy.

Plants have other beneficial properties too. Studies show that the scent of the Jasmine plant can reduce anxiety levels and also improve sleep quality. Lavender has been proven to lower heart rate, blood pressure and stress levels. Peace Lily, as well as being an amazing air cleaner, can increase room humidity by 5%. Increased humidity is great for breathing while asleep. Apartment Therapy Website – the lifestyle blog and home design website – says, "Low humidity causes static electricity, dry skin and hair, increased susceptibility to colds and respiratory illness and allows germs and viruses to thrive".

However, you do not want humidity to be above 60% or you can grow mould, and mould is toxic to your health. Naturally found outdoors, mould spores can easily enter your home through doorways, windows and air conditioning systems. Spores in the air can also be carried by people and animals. A musty smell is a sign that you have mould in your house. Also, you may see mould on walls or floors. The most common causes of mould are high humidity, condensation and water leaks (which can often be hidden inside the wall). Even brand-new homes can harbour mould as builders hastily install water damaged materials like dry wall, which is then covered by plaster and paint thus hiding its dirty secret. Mould in your home can make you sick, especially if you have allergies or asthma. Whether or not you are allergic, mould exposure can irritate your eyes, skin, nose, throat and lungs. Toxic black mould can even kill you if you are exposed for long enough as it produces mycotoxins that can shut down your organs, incapacitate your Immune system and damage your brain. Some of the symptoms of mould infection are brain fog, memory problems, trouble focussing, headaches, fatigue and weakness, unexplained muscle cramping, aches and pains in the joints, persistent nerve pain, numbness and tingling, hot flushes or sweats, appetite swings and blood sugar deregulation, imbalanced hormones and thyroid disorders, diabetes, hot eye problems like red eyes or light sensitivity, asthma and sinus problems like cough or shortness of breath. Mycotoxins can be found in urine samples of people who have been exposed to a mouldy environment. So, if you suspect your home or workplace is mouldy you can see your doctor for testing. There are ways you can decrease mould exposure: - fix plumbing leaks and other water problems as soon as possible. Discard absorbent or porous materials such as damp ceiling tiles and carpet if they become mouldy. If walls grow mould the drywall should be cut out and replaced. You can clean mould off hard surfaces such as solid wood furniture with vinegar and essential oils like clove and tea tree. Clean and repair roof gutters regularly, keep air conditioning drip pans and drain lines clear. Keep indoor humidity between 30% and 50% as this minimises mould growth. Do not dry wet clothes on radiators.

A major part of the body's immune response system is inflammation. Infections, wounds and any damage to tissue would not be able to heal without an inflammatory response. The signs and symptoms of inflammation can be uncomfortable but show that the body is trying to heal itself.

There are two types of inflammation, Acute and Chronic.
Acute is caused by harmful bacteria or tissue injury, the onset is usually rapid, and duration is a few days when inflammation should improve, turns into an abscess or it will become chronic. Symptoms of acute inflammation are pain, redness, immobility, swelling and heat. These signs only apply to inflammation of the skin. If inflammation occurs deep inside of the body, such as an internal organ, only some of the signs may be noticeable. For example, some internal organs may not have sensory nerve endings nearby so there will be no pain such as certain types of lung inflammation. Examples of diseases, conditions and situations that can result in acute inflammation include acute bronchitis, infected in-growing toenail, a sore throat from a cold or flu, a scratch or cut on the skin, high-intensity exercise, acute appendicitis, dermatitis, tonsillitis, infective meningitis, sinusitis and physical trauma.

Chronic Inflammation is caused by pathogens that the body cannot break down, including some types of virus, foreign bodies that remain in the system, failure to eliminate what was causing acute inflammation, an autoimmune disorder that attacks normal healthy tissue mistaking it for a pathogen that causes disease and exposure to a low level of a particular irritant, such as industrial chemical over a long period. The onset is slow from months to years which results in tissue death and thickening and scarring of connective tissue. Here are some examples of diseases and conditions that involve chronic inflammation: asthma, chronic peptic ulcer, tuberculosis, rheumatoid arthritis, periodontitis, ulcerative colitis and Chrohn's disease, sinusitis and active hepatitis. Symptoms of chronic inflammation present in a different way to acute inflammation and these can include fatigue, mouth sores, chest pain, abdominal pain, fever, rash and joint pain. Although damaged tissue cannot heal without inflammation, chronic inflammation can eventually cause several diseases and conditions including some cancers, rheumatoid arthritis, atherosclerosis, periodontitis and hay fever.

Inflammation needs to be well managed and here are some tips to reduce it:
Eat a good diet avoiding foods that are processed as they usually contain added sugar, salt, Tran's fats and preservatives.

Exercise regularly because this keeps your body moving and joints lubricated, it keeps muscles toned and your energy high.
Make sure you rest and get enough sleep.

Drink plenty of water.

Stop smoking.

The list of cancer-causing suspects continues and is daunting, but these days most of us are aware that poor diet, excessive alcohol consumption, lack of exercise and obesity are all contributing factors to long term ill health.
Obesity and overweight are major risk factors for a number of chronic

diseases including diabetes, cardiovascular disease and cancer. Obesity has reached epidemic proportions globally with at least 2.8 million people a year dying as a result of being overweight or obese.

A simple way to calculate your own BMI is as follows:

Multiply your weight in pounds by 703.

Multiply your height in inches by itself.

Divide the figure you got from step 1 by the answer you got in step 2.

This is your Body Mass Index. BMI

If you want to calculate in metric units:

Divide your weight (kgs) by your height (m)

Divide your answer from 1 by your height again

A person with a BMI of 30 or more is generally considered to be obese and a person with a BMI equal to more than 25 is considered overweight.

Here are some shocking facts about obesity: worldwide obesity has nearly tripled since 1975, in 2016 more than 1.9 billion adults 18 years and older were overweight and of these over 650 million were obese. Most of the world's population live in countries where overweight and obesity kills more people than underweight. 41 million children under the age of 5 were overweight or obese in 2016 and over 340 million children and adolescents aged 5-19 were overweight or obese. We know that being obese can add to the risk of cancer and other illnesses and eating the wrong foods is the main problem.

So, what is good food and what is bad food? Again, there is no simple answer, it is much more complex than that. If your immune system is functioning well then you can get away with eating what is referred to as bad food every now and again. However, if you are ill and your immune system is already compromised then you need to stick to good foods. Foods that are natural and easily digestible to take the strain away from your gut. Your gut is the most important factor in all illness. Here is a simple version of what pertains to foods you should avoid and foods you should eat more of to keep your gut healthy:

Foods which are processed and have added salt, sugar and contain preservatives and other chemicals are food you should avoid.

Fruits, vegetables and foods high in fibre, are foods you should eat more of as they are good for gut health and will reduce the risk of obesity.

By now you are probably nearing overload of information, so I'll offer here a lay-by.

Knowing what's good and bad is a very good start to making things better. This information will help you to decide to side-step potential problems and choose healthier options by simply watching and taking more notice of those things that aren't helping you. You don't have to change overnight – you got to where you are now over many years and just making a start to change is all you need to do – you don't need to peel the onion all in one go, and you certainly do not want to throw away all those layers of what made you who you are today. Step by step and layer by layer is the way to lasting positive change.

There's one thing missing on the list, which in my view is the biggest cause of cancer and other illnesses, more than anything else – stress. Even doctors agree that stress accounts for over 90% of illness. Some research institutions suggest that there are a number of ways that chronic stress can actually kill you. That includes increased levels of cortisol, which interfere with learning and memory, lower immune function and bone density, and increased blood pressure, cholesterol and heart disease.
What is stress? The best place to start is to view it from a biological perspective.

Humans, like all other organisms, have to interact with their environment to fulfil their needs. Stress is what happens when we are faced with the challenges in our environment. It is important for us to experience challenges as this is how we learn and adapt to our environment, and so stress can be healthy and natural. An example of the beneficial aspects of stress can be seen in the effects of exercise on muscle growth. When muscle cells are stressed, such as when we exercise, they become enlarged, and the muscles become stronger and better able to perform their tasks in future. When we are faced with a stressful situation, pathways in our body are activated to produce a stress response. This response is called the "fight, flight or freeze" response and is initiated in the brain when we perceive a situation as threatening. In nature, a stressor could involve being faced with a predator that threatens life. The stress response is designed to provide an individual with the best chances of getting out of a dangerous situation like escaping from the predator. This response is mainly generated by the sympathetic nervous system (SNS) and the hypothalamic pituitary adrenal (HPA) axis. The SNS and the parasympathetic nervous system (PNS) form part of the autonomic nervous system (ANS) of the body. The ANS helps keep the body in balance. In stressful situations, the SNS prepares the body to respond to the stressor through changes such as increased heart rate, increased breathing rate, enhanced mental alertness, increased blood flow to the muscle cells and decreased blood flow to the digestive system. The PNS is active when the body is in a relaxed state. It helps conserve energy and to support processes such as digestion and immune function. The HPA axis involves a cascade of hormones, with the end result being the release of cortisol from the adrenal glands. Cortisol helps the body to deal with stress by releasing energy stores and altering the immune and inflammatory responses. The stress response essentially redirects energy and focus to the systems in the body required to survive the stressful situation, and away from other ongoing processes in the body such as growth, digestion, and reproductive function. The components of the "fight, flight or freeze" response are vital for survival. It becomes a problem, however, when these symptoms get activated too frequently or for too long and the body remains in an activated state during which it loses balance or homeostasis – equilibrium. Stress that is severe, prolonged or frequent can have negative effects on our health and this is known as chronic stress. In everyday life, we are all faced with multiple challenges such as traffic congestion, academic or work stress, conflict in our relationships, financial problems, crime in our communities etc. This can lead to repeated activation of the stress response, which is meant to be a short-term response to help us out of a crisis situation. This is exactly what happened to me when I was young. I lived in a constant state of stress, and I am in no doubt that it was the stress that caused my ongoing health problems. It is now known that stress not only sends the human immune system into overdrive it can also wreak havoc on the trillions of bacteria that work and thrive inside our digestive system. Without the right balance of gut bacteria, the body cannot maintain good health. Remember over 70% of your immune system is in your gut and there are probably 100 trillion bacteria in the average human, 90% of which live mainly in the intestine. No wonder the focus is changing. Michael Bailey, an assistant professor of dentistry and member of the Institute for Behavioural Medicine Research at Ohio State University in the US has an interest in how stress affects bacteria naturally in our bodies. He and his colleagues turned to mice to better understand the role that bacteria play in immune balance. They ran a series of experiments using a common stressor for these animals. For two hours daily for six days, an aggressive mouse was placed in a cage of a group of more docile mice. At the end of the string of experiments, blood samples were taken from both stressed animals and matched mice from a control group, along with samples of material from inside each animal's intestine. The blood levels were analysed to detect the levels of two biomarkers used to gauge stress. From the intestinal samples Bailey's team could determine the relative proportion of at least 30 types of bacteria residing there. Compared to the control mice the stressed mice showed two marked differences: the proportion of one important type of bacteria in the gut – bacteroids – fell by 20% to 25% while another type - Clostridium – increased a similar amount. Also, levels of the two biomarkers IL-6 and MCP-1, jumped 10-fold in the stressed mice compared to the controls. The research then treated stressed mice with broad spectrum antibiotics that could kill as much as 90% of the intestinal bacteria for a short period. When they again looked at the two immune markets in the stressed mice, they saw only a doubling of IL-6 and MCP-1 - an increase only one fifth as much. "We know that if we knock the population of bacteria down with antibiotics, we don't have the same innate immune response," Bailey said. "That showed that the bacteria are involved in the ability of stress to prime the innate immune system." He said that the research showed that some of the changes in systemic immunity in the body can be influenced by changes in these bacterial colonies, a result that reinforces the idea that they have a broader effect on immune response.

Our response to stress is influenced by other factors as well, such as our thoughts and feelings about the challenges we face, and everyone is different. It will all depend, if you remember, on your life experiences and how your subconscious mind has been programmed to keep you safe. You can employ distraction techniques to help minimise the effect of everyday stressful situations. So, for example, if you are stuck in traffic and you listen to calming music you are less likely to become frustrated and will have less of a stress response than the person who becomes upset and angry. I will give you some more simple distraction techniques later on to help you to manage stress. However, if you want to deal with the cause, you need Onion Therapy. You see, it is not the situation that is stressful, it is how you respond to it. If it were the situation, then we would all be stressed about the same things, but we are not. What stresses me might not stress you and vice versa. The bad news is we can't always change the situation we are in; for example, if we have a stressful job, we might not be in a position to change it. The good news is we can always change the way we think and feel about it, and this is all we need to get rid of the symptoms. Simple? Not quite.

Dealing with the symptoms is one thing, but unless you deal with the cause the symptoms will keep coming back. However, the "quick fix" will help you manage stress in the moment, and it will certainly make a difference. Here are some techniques that will help you to change the way you feel about a stressful situation. They are distraction techniques and I use these myself.

A simple technique for removing negative thoughts.

Instead of trying to think positive, remove negative thoughts by practising and perfecting the following process:

Whenever a thought comes into your head ask yourself the question, "Is this thought going to benefit me?" If it isn't, then simply remove it from your thoughts. You may find this hard at first, especially if there is a lot going on in your life and you feel overwhelmed with negative thoughts and worries. To help to train your mind to slow down, take control of your thoughts and remove them easily, practice the following transitional technique; this is not the way to do it long term, but it will help you to start the process.

Whenever you have a negative thought think of something wonderful, maybe an experience you have had and think about it for 15 seconds. Initially you may find that you can only hold the thought for a few seconds but keep practising (at least 20-30 times every day) and soon it will become easy. You will notice how good you feel when you come out of it, and you may find that answers to your problems pop into your mind.

These techniques will help you to filter your thoughts automatically which means you will be able to eliminate negative thoughts instead of processing them. This technique needs a lot of practice, but it is very effective and is worth it.

Always remember that it is not the situation that causes you stress, it is the way you feel about it. It doesn't matter if you can't change the situation, you can always change the way you feel about it. Here are five simple ways:

1. Every morning when you wake up think of 5 things you are grateful for. Focus on what you have got rather than what you haven't. Smile when you are thinking about these things.

2. Close your eyes and spend 5-10 minutes sending love to someone or something you love. In order to send love, you have to feel love, so this is perfect for those of you who have low self-esteem and do not love yourself.

3. Close your eyes, relax, and think about a specific time when you were really happy, very calm, peaceful, feeling good about yourself and totally stress free. For example, it might be a lovely hollday. Go back there and visualise that holiday in every detail using all of your senses. Think of who was there, what they looked like, what they were wearing and the colours. Think of what they said. Think of the location, where it was, the colours of the sky, sea, and surrounding area, the feel of the wind, the sound of the birds, the smell of the sea, etc. Remember how good you

felt and where you felt it. It is important to recall the event with all of your senses so that it feels just like it did when you were there. This will trick your mind into feeling the same way that it did on that day, which will not only change how you feel, but it is so powerful it will also change the physiology of your body. Spend as long as you like on this exercise, you can do it anywhere, anytime and it is really good to do if you are feeling stressed and anxious.

4. Practice finding a positive in every negative. So, for example, if your car won't start in the morning and you have to call out the breakdown service, which will make you late for work: think about how lucky you were that it happened at home and not while you were out at night. The time you have to wait is useful time in which you can prepare your evening meal, which will free up more time to relax later on.

5. Laugh! Yes laugh. Making yourself laugh will trick your body into thinking it is happy and "laughter is the best medicine" for doing that. You can do this anytime anywhere and once again it will not only change your mood but also the physiology of your body. Laughter is infectious so if you start laughing then others will laugh too. They might think you're mad, but they probably think that anyway! If you can't bring yourself to do this, watch comedy shows or funny films, anything that will make you laugh. Try it, it is so easy to do and yet it will make you feel so much better.

The Lady With the Lamp
(Saint Filomena)

Whene'er a noble deed is wrought
Whene'er is spoken a noble thought
Our hearts in glad surprise,
To higher levels rise.

The tidal wave of deeper souls

Into our inmost being rolls,
And lifts us unawares
Out of all meaner cares.

Honour to those whose words or deeds
Thus help us in our daily needs,
And by their overflow
Raise us from what is low!

Thus thought I, as by night I read
Of all the great army of the dead,
The trenches cold and damp,
The starved and frozen camp,

The wounded from the battle-plain
In dreary hospitals of pain,
The cheerless corridors,
The cold and stony floors.

Lo! In that house of misery
A lady with a lamp I see
Pass through the glimmering of gloom
And flit from room to room.

And slow, as in a dream of bliss,
The speechless sufferer turns to kiss
Her shadow, as it falls
Upon the darkening of walls.

As if a door in heaven should be
Opened and then closed suddenly,
The vision came and went,
The light shone and was spent.

On England's annals, through the long
Hereafter of her speech and song,

That light its rays shall cast
From portals of the past.
A lady with a lamp shall stand
In the great history of the land,
A noble type of good,
Heroic womanhood.

Nor even shall be wanting here
The palm, the lily, and the spear,
The symbols that of yore
Saint Filomena bore.

Henry Wadsworth Longfellow

Chapter 11

What About the Carers?

The number of people caring for someone with cancer in the UK is, according to the organisation Caring UK, 6.8 million and is rising year on year to such an extent that it is estimated that by the 2030s it will reach in excess of 9 million people. And yet they get little or no direct organised support. The patient always comes first, but a cancer diagnosis has as much of an impact on a carer as it does on the person with cancer. Carers need support too! At the Cancer Self-Help Group Loughborough, we always include them. They can attend our meetings and social events and have access to everything we provide for people who have cancer. Meeting with other carers allows them to share their experiences, good and bad, and it provides a forum for them to talk about how they feel, which they say is a massive help. A problem shared is a problem halved. But it is not just group support they need, they need the support of other family members, friends and healthcare providers; caring is a tremendous burden physically, mentally and emotionally. Caring for someone with cancer can mean taking on the day to day running of the house including washing, ironing, shopping and cooking; something they may not ever have done before. Often this is in conjunction with trying to hold down a job, too. Carers are often the ones that co-ordinate medical and treatment appointments, as well as making sure that their loved one gets there on time. They may have to learn about the different medications and side effects, make sure these are taken on time and that repeat prescriptions are ordered and collected so nothing runs out. As if that isn't enough, they have to try and keep upbeat and positive even when the patient, usually someone they love, takes out their anger and frustration on them. This is so stressful and often carers themselves become physically ill as a result.

This lack of support was the subject of research carried out by Postavaru, Munir, McDermott, Ahmed and Fathers in 2018. The study was partly funded by the British Psychological Society and their conclusions identified physical and psychological challenges associated with the care role and responsibilities. The evidence supports the value of specialist services and the need for more inclusive and family-oriented services, where healthcare practitioners engage in discussion with patients and their carers to advise on how to manage the illness throughout the diagnostic and treatment journey. Hopefully this type of research will help to bring about changes in the healthcare system. Doctors please note that one of the items that came up in the study was how, where, when, and by whom, was the person with cancer given their diagnosis. I urge you to think carefully about how you do this; if it is done well, it can make a big difference to the person's health journey.

We have already talked about the patient and the carer being honest with each other and sharing their thoughts and feelings. If you have cancer don't shut your loved one out, include them and tell them what you want. Tell them what your decision is, in terms of whether or not to have treatment or if you want to take the conventional or alternative approach or a combination of both. Carers, doctors and family, please respect the wishes of the patient and support them, even if it is not something that you believe in. By all means give them your opinion but don't try to force them to do what you think is right. Difficult I know, but it is their journey and not yours and it will only make things more stressful for them if you put pressure on them to change their mind.

A good example of this was my friend Kate, who was diagnosed with advanced breast cancer and decided not to have any treatment and to take the holistic approach. She changed her diet and lifestyle and began to live life to the full. However, her father was a doctor, and he believed passionately that she should have chemotherapy. In trying to persuade her, he said that if she didn't have it, he would have nothing more to do with her. Presumably he thought that this would change her mind, but it didn't, and as a result she went through her entire journey without the support of her family. Kate lived alone with her devoted chocolate Labrador who remained with her until she died, even having pride of place at her funeral. Fortunately, she had many friends who helped and supported her throughout. They even took it in turns to stay with her day and night until she died making sure she was never alone. So please think about this when you feel like putting pressure on your loved one to do what you believe is right. Support is what they need, especially when they are not going to get better, and they want to die.

It is appropriate here to explore the final choice – an acceptance of the inevitable – Death is an Option.

*　　*　　*

A Song of Living

Because I have loved life, I shall have no sorrow to die.
I have sent up my gladness on wings, to be lost in the blue
of the sky,
I have run and leaped with the rain, I have taken the wind

to my breast.
My cheeks like a drowsy child to the face of the earth I
have pressed.
Because I have loved life, I shall have no sorrow to die.

I have kissed young love on the lips, I have heard his song
to the end,
I have struck my hand like a seal in the loyal hand of a
friend.
I have known the peace of heaven, the comfort of work
done well.
I have longed for death in the darkness and risen alive out
of hell.
Because I have loved life, I shall have no sorrow to die.

I gave a share of my soul to the world, when and where my
course is run.
I know that another shall finish the task I surely must leave
undone.
I know that no flower, nor flint was in vain on the path I
trod.
As one looks on a face through a window, through life I
have looked on God,
Because I have loved life, I shall have no sorrow to die.

Amelia Josephine Burr

Chapter 12

Death is an Option

Before I start, I am going to state the obvious – we are all going to die! Fact!   Death is a part of our life, but we avoid talking about it, planning for it and celebrating it. The main reason is fear, fear of the unknown.

However, beliefs form a big part too. My Auntie May was a devout Catholic who believed without question that if she lived a good life, when she died, she would go to heaven. So, she wasn't afraid. I envy people like my Auntie May, as I fit into the category of those who would like to believe but are not sure. Everyone has their own beliefs, but no one can really know what it is like to die unless they have experienced it. There are a few people who have had near death experiences, and I have read many of their stories which all seem to have a lot in common.

It wasn't until I read Anita Moorjani's book, 'Dying to be me' that my belief changed, and I can honestly say that I no longer fear death, although I do still worry about the process. The way Anita explains what it was like when she died is so beautifully written and it conjures up a picture of total bliss, love, joy and happiness. Instead of being afraid of death it is something to look forward to. Her take on it tied in with my own beliefs which are very different to those of my Auntie May. We are all made up of energy and energy resonates at different levels. For example water, ice and steam are all the same thing but because the energy levels are different, they appear in a different form; I believe the same applies to human beings and that while we are in our physical bodies we are in the solid form, but when we die, we leave those physical bodies and we resonate at a higher level, a level that cannot be seen but can be felt. How many of you have lost loved ones and yet sense they are still there? I know I have. How many have asked loved ones who have died for help with a problem and suddenly you get the answer. These are just a couple of examples, and I am sure that some of you can come up with many more. But it does depend on what you believe; if you think what I believe is an utter load of rubbish then your explanation for these things will be totally different. Now I will ask you a question: whatever you believe happens to us when we die, do you truly believe it? This makes a difference as most of us want to believe in something after this life is ended, just as I used to do, but there is still that element of doubt. If you believe totally, you are fearless. So, what can you do if you don't truly believe? Change your belief! How do you do that, well for a start try reading Anita's book. This book is for anyone: young adults, working age with families, looking at retirement and beyond. Death also becomes more of a focus if you have been diagnosed with a life limiting disease such as cancer, or if you have had cancer and are in remission, because in my experience, most people live in fear of the cancer coming back. If that is the case then the fear of it coming back and the fear of dying cause you to live in a constant state of stress, which as we know is the cause of 90% of physical illnesses. So, what else can we do to take away the fear of death? Plan it! As I've said before, it is a fact that those who have a 'terminal' illness and who have made a plan B in case they do not get well, live longer than those who don't. Why is that? I am afraid I don't have the answer, but at least it puts you in control and being out of control is one of the biggest causes of stress. During my time as a volunteer with the Cancer Self Help Group, I have learned that when people are really ill there comes a time when they themselves want to die. They are tired; they have had enough and yet they hang on and keep on trying all the medications, diets and therapies for the sake of their family. I will never forget the time when one of the members of the group who attended with her partner told me in confidence that she just wanted to die; she had had enough, but she didn't want to tell her partner who was desperately trying to keep her alive. I know it is hard, but it is important to let your loved ones know that this is your wish, hard as it is. Then you are at one with yourself and your loved ones. What I would urge you to do, if you haven't done so already, is to make your plan B. Plan your death. Where do you want to die, what do you want to happen when you die, have you made a will, do you want to be buried or cremated etc. etc. There are so many things that you need to plan so that your death is just how you want it and so that those left behind know exactly what your wishes are. These are all the things that prompted Patricia Byron to write her book called 'Last Orders'. Patricia was a friend of my friend Kate who had a very aggressive and advanced form of breast cancer. Kate chose not to have conventional treatment, choosing the holistic route instead, and she out-lived her prognosis by 5 years. However, Kate was on her own with no family support and the most important thing in her life was her chocolate Labrador, Ellie, who towards the end of her life never left her side. Patricia was appointed executor of Kate's will, but this wasn't the first time she had been an executor. A few years earlier she had been through the same thing with another friend, and also with her mum. When her friend and her mum passed away there were so many questions that had been left unanswered because they each had refused to talk about death. Patricia was left to choose whether they were buried or cremated, what they would like to be buried in and so on.   As with most families, people have different ideas of what the deceased would have wanted, and this can often cause a rift at a time when people should be supporting each other. So, when my friend Kate was given a 'terminal' prognosis Patricia tackled the subject and wrote 'Last Orders' for her. Kate was shocked to see it and they both shed many tears as Kate completed it, but it was important for Patricia to make sure she could do the best for her friend. That included everything surrounding her death, her funeral, her belongings, and her beloved dog.   Kate passed away peacefully at her home, just as she'd wanted, and I attended her funeral which was probably the best funeral I have ever been to. Her chocolate labrador was chief mourner and the service reflected her incredible sense of humour when she was brought into the church with 'Another one bites the dust' by Queen playing in the background. Everything went without a single hitch; Kate would have loved it and I feel sure she was there watching it.   'Last Orders' is a superb book that can be completed by anyone at any time, but why not do it when you are healthy and feeling upbeat? After all, that's usually the time when we make our will.   I have bought a copy of the book, completed it and I've told Mike where it is for when something happens to me.   Naturally I review it as things change but the fundamentals will remain the same.

*   *   *

A Modern Version of the Hippocratic Oath

I swear to fulfil, to the best of my ability and judgement,
this covenant:

I will respect the hard-won scientific gains of those physicians in whose steps I walk, and gladly share such knowledge as is mine with those who are to follow.

I will apply, for the benefit of the sick, all measures which are required, avoiding those twin traps of overtreatment and therapeutic nihilism.

I will remember that there is an art to medicine as well as science, and that warmth, sympathy, and understanding may outweigh the surgeon's knife or the chemist's drug.

I will not be ashamed to say, "I know not," nor will I fail to call in my colleagues when the skills of another are needed for a patient's recovery.

I will respect the privacy of my patients, for their problems are not disclosed to me that the world may know.

Most especially must I tread with care in matters of life and death. If it is given to me to save a life, all thanks. But it may also be within my power to take a life; this awesome responsibility must be faced with great humbleness and awareness of my own frailty. Above all, I must not play at God.

I will remember that I do not treat a fever chart, a cancerous growth, but a sick human being, whose illness may affect the person's family and economic stability. My responsibility includes these related problems, if I am to care adequately for the sick.

I will prevent disease whenever I can, for prevention is preferable to cure.

I will remember that I remain a member of society, with

special obligations to all my fellow human beings, those sound of mind and body as well as the infirm.

If I do not violate this oath, may I enjoy life and art, respected while I live and remembered with affection thereafter.

May I always act so as to preserve the finest traditions of my calling and may I long experience the joy of healing those who seek my help.

The modern version of the Hippocratic Oath was written in 1964 by Louis Lasagna, Dean of the School of Medicine at Tufts University.

Chapter 13

Doctors read this!

Doctors when you are faced with a patient who has cancer by all means give them a diagnosis but please, please, do not give them a prognosis.

I appreciate it is not easy for you to make a diagnosis when patients present with an array of symptoms, and you only have 10 minutes to decide what to do. However, you will be pleased to know that Dr Ben Noble, a GP at our local Woodbrook surgery in Loughborough, has joined forces with his dad to invent a new online mind-mapping tool that helps doctors speed up cancer diagnosis. This is very important because as you know the earlier cancer is detected the easier it is to treat. The innovative 'Cancer Maps 'were developed to help make it easier for GPs to navigate the cancer recognition and referral guidelines published by the National Institute for Health and Care Excellence (NICE) in 2015. This mind-mapping tool has so impressed the medical community that it has been endorsed by NICE and the Royal College of GPs and will soon be rolled out across the UK. It will also help train GPs and other health professionals through Gateway C**, an online cancer education for primary care.

The Cancer Maps consist of three different, brightly coloured maps covering different organs of the body. The interactive tool is intended largely for use by GPs as an aid during consultations. If the doctor suspects cancer, the patients age, sex and symptoms are keyed in and areas of the maps will light up, flagging potential routes for action. Results can be clearly seen by both doctor and patient alike, reassuring patients that the right steps are being taken.

As well as highlighting when a referral ought to be made – for example a chest X-ray, a scan or an urgent referral for suspected cancer – the user can also click on the relevant pathway for more detailed information about the NICE guidelines.

Over half (53%) of the GPs who tested the pilot Cancer Maps said using the tool during consultations prompted them to refer a patient for further investigation when they otherwise might not have done. Feedback also showed that the great majority of the GPs (94%) indicated they would recommend the tool to healthcare professionals and 9 out of 10 GPs said they felt more confident about making cancer referrals. I have seen the tool and I am very impressed with it. I know it is going to have a massive impact and will help to reassure patients and GPs thus alleviating some of the stress involved for both parties.
Here is a link:
https://www.gatewayc.org.uk/cancer-maps/ *

To be diagnosed with cancer, what it is, where it is and what stage it is at, gives patients a starting point, a label and something that they can research for information, both conventional and complementary. It gives them choice and control which is very important in their healing journey. Everyone is different and we see that at the Cancer Group. Some choose to go the conventional route, some the complementary route and some a mixture of both. Some have been told there is nothing more conventional medicine can do and so the only alternative for them is the complementary route which gives them hope again. Whatever they choose please respect that it is their choice and support them, even if you don't believe in what they are doing. In addition, when you diagnose their cancer, please give them the options that traditional medicine can offer but do not pressurise them into deciding quickly. Let them go away to process what you have told them, give them breathing space so that they can do some research and ask some questions before they decide on the best course of treatment for them. This is important as often we have members who come to our group who have had radiotherapy and/or chemotherapy who, if they had known what they now know would not have had it. Others say they would have still chosen to have it, as they believe it was the right thing to do, given the circumstances. The founder of our group, Joyce Walton is one. She had surgery and radiotherapy for her ovarian cancer and the radio therapy has left her with damaged lungs as well as other side effects. At the time, given the information available, she had felt it was worth taking the risk in order to save her life. However, she combined conventional treatment with complementary treatments which at the time were almost unheard of. She was lucky enough to have the support of her doctors which made a huge difference. In fact, when she got better despite all the odds, her doctors wanted to know more about what she had done. It is a fact that those who have their doctors' support do much better than those who do not and are pressurised into having treatments they do not want. I hear stories from members who have been told by their doctor that if they do not have chemotherapy they will die. I think this is appalling - it is never that certain that whatever you have will kill you. At our group alone we have members who have chosen not to have any medical treatment at all, and they have outlived the prognosis they have been given. You can find hundreds of examples of this if you look, so please do not frighten people into thinking they will die if they don't do what you believe is the right thing. I know it is hard, as you believe you are doing what is right, based on the information you have been given whilst in training and since. However, most of your training was to do with what medication to prescribe for a particular illness, and there are more and more drugs coming to market by the day. The pharmaceutical industry is worth billions and needs to make a profit, so much of the information out there is geared to allow them to do just that. Trials which have been done that do not give them the information they want are hidden, while trials that seem to show that a drug works are promoted everywhere to validate what they say about the drug. It all seems to make sense as the research and trials are done by eminent medics in their field, so we believe it. But, if you look closely, many of the medics who conduct the trials and write these reports are employed by the pharmaceutical industry. There is a lot of information out there that we are not given but if you look carefully, you can find it. Take Statins for example. These are the so-called wonder drugs, widely prescribed to lower blood cholesterol levels and they claim to offer unparalleled protection against heart disease. Believed to be completely safe and capable of preventing a whole series of other conditions, they are the most profitable drug in the history of medicine. In his ground-breaking book, 'The Great Cholesterol Con' GP Malcolm Kendrick exposes the truth behind the hype, revealing that high cholesterol levels don't cause heart disease and a high-fat diet – saturated or otherwise – does not affect blood cholesterol levels. The protection provided by statins is so small as to be not worth bothering about for most men and women and statins have more side effects than has been admitted. Their advocates should be treated with scepticism due to their links with the manufacturers. Everything he talks about in the book can be backed up with scientific evidence, things that have been hidden from us. If this can happen with statins then it can, and does, happen with other drugs and treatments. Scary don't you think? And if the doctors don't know the truth, then what hope is there for the rest of us!

Now I am going to ask you: when you became a doctor you signed the Hippocratic Oath? And Hippocrates was the father of medicine, wasn't he? He said a lot of things which are all bound up in the Hippocratic Oath which you sign when you become a doctor. One of which is "let food be thy medicine, let medicine be thy food". Whatever happened to that? How much training did you get in nutrition when you trained to be a doctor? Very little I am told, sometimes less than an hour and yet it is fundamental to health. As you know, over 70% of your immune system is in the gut, so doesn't it make sense that the focus of health should be on the gut. That means nutrition and making sure that by eating a healthy diet you are giving it all the nutrients that it needs to function properly. A healthy gut means a healthy immune system and a healthy immune system can fight off viruses and infections all by itself. So, no need for drugs!

Here are some other quotes from Hippocrates:
I will prevent disease whenever I can for prevention is better than cure.

Natural forces within us are the true healers of disease.
If we could give every individual the right amount of nourishment and exercise, not too little and not too much, we would have found the safest way to health.

Science is the father of knowledge, but opinion breeds ignorance.

Make a habit of two things – to help, or at least do no harm.

Let's just look at that last one for a minute, what did he mean by harm? Well that depends on what your beliefs are, but I am playing devil's advocate here. Could chemotherapy fall into that category? After all chemotherapy is mustard gas, a chemical used to kill people in the First World War. If it can kill people in the war, then why are we giving it to people with cancer?
Well, because it will kill cancer cells.

Of course, it will, it will kill everything including the immune system that is there to fight disease. So why are we killing that off, does it make sense to you? When doctors say they have killed off all of the cancer, how can this be? In order to kill off all of the cancer you need to kill all of the person surely, or there is still a chance the cancer will come back. That is exactly what happens in most cases and if you look at the statistics, they support this. Cancer comes back some time later, often in a different place. Of course, when you administer chemotherapy, you have to be very careful with the dose because if you give too much it will kill the patient in no time – although when that happens it's not the chemotherapy that killed them it is the cancer. I know this doesn't happen in all cases because people are different and there are those who have had chemotherapy who have got well and have remained well. Why is that? Well could it be in addition to having chemotherapy they changed their lifestyle took more care of their diet, exercised more and lived life to the full – in fact all of the things that Hippocrates advocates. Just a thought because there are so many variables. But here is a thing, given that chemotherapy can be a gruelling and miserable therapy, why do doctors advise people to have it just in case or when they are receiving palliative care? The answer is to extend their life for a few weeks or months. If you are facing death, depending on your beliefs, you will grab at anything that will give you some extra time. However, often that time is a time of suffering, a time when you cannot enjoy the life you still have left and often the treatment itself has to be stopped because your body cannot take any more. All of our members that I've spoken to, who have lost loved ones who chose chemotherapy to extend their life, said with hindsight they made the wrong decision. Tells you something, doesn't it? Doctors, what would you do? Would you have chemotherapy yourself? It might surprise you to know that a study done amongst doctors in the USA came back with 85% of doctors saying they wouldn't have chemotherapy and nor would they advise their family to have it.

Something else you may not know, which I think you should, is that chemotherapy is not going to work on all types of cancers and the only way you can find out is by having a genetic profile done. How do I know? One of our members, Leela and David Mitchelson's son Glyn, had a very rare form of cancer. He was encouraged to have chemotherapy and then immunotherapy when the chemotherapy didn't work. The chemotherapy ruined his thyroid function and gave him other nasty life changing side effects too. It was gruelling and the regime left him very weak. When nothing worked, Leela and David paid £1800.00 pounds to have a genetic profile done as it is not available on the National Health Service. They were as shocked as I was by the results. The chemotherapy and immunotherapy would never have worked on his type of cancer. So, he had gone through all of the pain and suffering for nothing and was left weak and ill as a result. If he had been given the option of having a genetic profile done, he would not have chosen to have chemotherapy in the first place. Even if the test is not available on the National Health Service, at least it is information that people should know in order to make an informed choice. Sadly, Glyn died on 18th November 2018 at the age of 37.

I am not saying that people should not have chemotherapy, I am saying they should have access to all the information available before they make that choice. Even if they survive the chemotherapy, and the cancer is in remission, they are often left with terrible side effects. So, it is a big decision to make. There is no doubt that some people who have chemotherapy get well, and their cancer doesn't come back, but I believe there are a lot of different reasons for this: It may be that they have changed their lifestyle and started to live life to the full, enjoying every minute of it, but everyone is different and there is much more that we don't yet understand. Never underestimate the power of belief; that is why I urge you as doctors never to give a prognosis because if people believe you, you have effectively given them a death sentence. I have witnessed this firsthand and many of our members who have lost loved ones will back me up. There are members of our group who had been told they only had 6 months maximum to live and, lo and behold, they died in 6 months. Why? Because they believed it. On the other hand, Joyce, who was also given that prognosis, didn't believe it and she is 87, still alive and has survived three separate cancers all of which were primary and not secondary (where the original cancer comes back in another place). I am not saying that belief is the only reason, but it seems to be a big factor in whether a person will get well or not, and whether a treatment will work or not.

So please, do not give anyone a prognosis, as you do not know how long someone is going to live. There are people like Joyce, who got better despite all the odds meaning it is possible for others to get better, too. If you want to read more of this, read 'Radical Remission, surviving cancer against all the odds' by Kelly A. Turner, Ph.D. In her book she identified nine key factors that can make a real difference. Remission from cancer is a clinical fact and, in her book, she shows how we can shift the odds of remission in our favour. It is a balanced book, and she does not ask anyone to abandon conventional therapy but instructs us how to add healing factors to the mix that are often overlooked.

So, doctors, think about what you say and how you say it to your patients. You have so much power and influence because they believe you. Most people accept what doctors say and believe that doctors know best. To some extent that is true, but not always the case. Do not take away hope as no matter how ill someone is, even if they are at death's door, there is always hope. This is exactly what happened to Anita Moorjani, who, after fighting cancer for four years, was in a coma. Her husband and family were called to her bedside as the hospital did not expect her to survive the night. As her organs failed, she entered into an extraordinary near-death experience where she realised her inherent worth and the actual cause of her disease. Upon regaining consciousness, Anita found that her condition had improved so rapidly that she could be released from hospital within weeks without a trace of cancer in her body. If that makes you think then I urge you to look on Chris Wark's website www.chrisbeatcancer.com where you will find lots of case studies of people who have got well despite the odds. Just because we don't hear about these people doesn't mean to say they are not out there. They are and I'm sure there are many more examples of people who have survived cancer against all the odds, which have not been documented.

Doctors, I hope by reading this, it has made you think about things that you might not have thought about before, and to rethink what, and how, you say things to your patients. Be careful not to impose your opinion on them just like Dr Hilary Jones did when he appeared on Lorraine, a morning TV program in the UK. He referred to reflexology as 'mumbo jumbo'. He is a medical professional, a doctor, and to say something like this without doing any research first is highly damaging. Anyone watching that program may have as a result, missed out on trying something that may have been very beneficial. Indeed, Dr Ranjan Chatterjee, in his book The Stress Solution, says the opposite and encourages people to try reflexology. He says that studies have shown that this gentle and relaxing therapy can help reduce levels of the stress hormone cortisol. He says that many of his patients have reported back to him that reflexology helps to lower their stress levels and improve their sleep quality. In addition, what Dr Jones would have found out, if he had done some research before, he made that statement, is that NICE the National Institute for Care and Clinical Excellence in the UK, in 2003, approved reflexology for pain relief in people who have Multiple Sclerosis. To quote Hippocrates again, "Science is the father of knowledge but opinion breeds ignorance." There have not been many scientific studies done into the effectiveness of reflexology, but I know from my own experience, and from the feedback from my clients, that it does relieve stress and it does improve sleep quality. So, if doctors agree that over 90% of all illnesses are caused by stress then it is a no brainer to encourage people to use any therapy, method or technique that will reduce stress.

Now we are nearing the end of the book but as I have constantly said throughout, "Information is Power", so the next chapter is all about resources you can access which include books, websites and links. Make sure you spend time researching your particular cancer on the internet and the various conventional and alternative treatments available and also look to see if you are eligible for any trials that are taking place. Take a look at the different diets people have adopted, select the one that resonates with you and stick to it, don't try to combine them all. Go with your "gut instinct" and choose what feels right for you. Try to incorporate complementary therapies; if you can't afford them and you have cancer look for support groups that offer them free.
Make time for hobbies that will distract and relax you but most

importantly learn how to manage and deal with fear by using the power of your mind and changing your beliefs. This is the most important element you must address in order to give yourself the best chance to fully heal.

* * *

Knowledge

*Now that I know
That passion warms little
Of flesh in the mold,
And treasure is brittle,*

*I'll lie here and learn
How, over their ground,
Trees make a long shadow
And a light sound.*

By Louise Bogan

Chapter 14

Resources Section

Information Is Power

In this section you will find a lot of information but as you know, I like to keep things simple so where do you start?   Initially, I have listed a few of what, in my opinion, are excellent resources. These will cover a mixture of things: books, websites, therapies, therapies I have tried, books I have read, websites I subscribe to and diets etc. These are the things that I would suggest you look at first as this will give you a quick overview of things you need to know. I haven't put links to specific cancers as there are so many and everyone will be different. This is something you will have to do yourself.   So, when the doctor gives you, a diagnosis make a point of finding out all you can about your particular cancer, the treatments available and if there are any trials that you might be eligible for.   This, together with my information will provide you with a starting point, from then on it is your choice if you want to find out more.

If you do, you will find a comprehensive list of resources in this chapter which are just some of resources that I have amassed over 10 years; books I have read and books we have in our library at The Cancer Self-help Group.   These are just the tip of the iceberg! Things are constantly being changed, updated and added, but this will give you enough to be going on with without having to do much research yourself.   I am always on the internet looking for information, but that is my passion - it may not be yours which is why I have tried to make it easy for you.

Therapies
REFLEXOLOGY

This was the first complementary therapy I was introduced to when I was really ill many years ago; after only one treatment I felt a big difference in both my stress and energy levels, and I also slept better. I still have reflexology regularly and would highly recommend it for stress relief.

If you are looking for a qualified and regulated practitioner have a look on the Association of Reflexologists Website: https://www.aor.org.uk

I trained with the International Institute of Reflexology – The Only School Licensed to Teach the Original Ingham Method of Reflexology: https://www.reflexology-uk.net

Books

Stories the Feet Can Tell Thru Reflexology Stories the Feet Have Told Thru Reflexology,
Eunice D. Ingham; Dwight C Byers
Eunice Ingham – A Biography, Christine Issel
Better Health with Foot Reflexology, Dwight Byers
Hand Reflexology, Michael and Louise Keet
Reflexology Success at The Last Resort By Diane and Paul Breeding
Clinical Reflexology A Guide for Health Professionals, Edited by Peter A Mackereth Denise Tiran

REIKI

I trained with Penny Quest (now retired), if you want to find a practitioner or if you want to learn Reiki yourself look on the UK Reiki Federation website: https://www.reikifed.co.uk

Books

Reiki for Life - The Complete Guide to Reiki Practice for Levels 1, 2 and 3 by Penelope Quest
Self - Healing with Reiki: How to create wholeness, harmony and balance for body, mind and spirit by Penelope Quest
The Reiki Manual: A Training Guide for Reiki Students, Practitioners and

Masters by Penelope Quest, Kathy Roberts
The Original Reiki Handbook of Dr Mikao Usui: The Traditional Usui Reiki Ryoho Treatment Positions and Numerous Reiki Techniques for Health and Well-being by Mikao Usui, Frank Arjava Petter
Reiki the Healing Touch: First and Second Degree Manual by William Rand
The Spirit of Reiki the complete handbook of the Reiki System Walter Lubeck Frank Arjava Petter William Lee Rand

EFT
Gary Craig is the original founder here is a link to his website: httpps://www.emofree.com
I trained with Karl Dawson EFT & Matrix Reimprinting; here is a link to his website:
https://www.matrixreimprinting.com/practitioner.aspx

Books
Matrix Reimprinting using EFT Rewrite Your Past Transform Your Future, Karl Dawson and Sash Allenby
The Healing Power of EFT & Energy Psychology, David Feinstein, Donna Eden & Gary Craig
Attracting Abundance with EFT, Carol Look, EFT Master
Improve Your Eyesight with EFT, Carol Look LCSW,DCH,EFT Master
The Tapping Solution, Nick Ortner
Tapping for Kids, by Angie Muccillo
Adventures in EFT, Silvia Hartman
The Advanced Patterns of EFT, Silvia Hartman

THE BOWEN TECHNIQUE
A gentle therapy that is applied to areas of the body using thumbs and fingers in a specific process or order and is designed to stimulate nerve pathways which allow 'communication' to take place between different nervous systems of the body, restoring and correcting imbalance within the patient. Musculoskeletal problems such as frozen shoulder, back and neck pain account for the majority of conditions brought for Bowen treatment, it can also be helpful with more organic problems. Clients have reported significant improvements with asthma, migraines, irritable bowel, infertility and other reproductive problems.

https://thebowentechnique.com/

Books and information on Cancer:
If you have just been diagnosed with cancer or if you know someone has just been diagnosed with cancer the first book you should read is:
The Topic of Cancer by Jessica Richards. There are chapters on how to cope with diagnosis, what questions to ask, how to manage your time, and choose your support network. There is a powerful section on positive thinking, and how to boost your mental strength, and a hugely practical section on diet, complete with recipes life enhancing and store-cupboard ideas. There are chapters on what to say to someone who has been diagnosed with cancer (and what not to say) and how to be a valuable source of help. All these are backed up with anecdotes and real-life experience from Jessica, shot through with her irrepressible and life enhancing humour.

The next books are motivational and show how anyone can get better from cancer no matter what stage it is at. These books will help you to change your beliefs and give you hope when that has been taken away:

Radical Remission Surviving Cancer Against All Odds by Kelly A. Turner, Ph.D. This book gives the results of Kelly's research on over a thousand cases of Radical Remission – people who have defied a serious or even terminal diagnosis with a complete reversal of the disease. The results of this study focused on seventy-five factors, include astounding insights of the nine key factors that she found among nearly every Radical Remission survivor she has studied and how you can put these practices to work in your life. Every chapter includes dramatic stories of survivors' journeys back to wellness.

Dying to be Me by Anita Moorjani. In this truly inspirational book memoir, Anita Moorjani relates how, after fighting cancer for almost four years, her body – overwhelmed by the malignant cells spreading through her system began shutting down. As her organs failed, she entered into an extraordinary near-death experience where she realised her inherent worth… and the actual cause of her disease. Upon regaining consciousness, Anita found that her condition had improved so rapidly that she could be released from the hospital within weeks ... without a trace of cancer in her body.

Anita has a website which I recommend you sign up to so that you can receive her newsletter and listen to her inspirational talks and question and answer sessions: www.anitamoorjani.com

Chris Beat Cancer by Chris Wark - At the age of 26 Chris was diagnosed with stage 3 colon cancer and before he knew it was having surgery to remove a golf ball sized tumour and one third of his colon. He refused chemotherapy and used nutrition and natural therapies to heal. His book is packed with intense personal insight and extensive healing solutions that will inspire and guide you on your own journey to wellness. Have a look at his website www.ChrisBeatCancer.com

Your Life in Your Hands by Professor Jane Plant. Professor Jane Plant suffered from breast cancer five times before she learned of the relationship between diet and disease.   As one of Britain's most eminent scientists, her revolutionary analysis of the underlying causes of breast cancer and her simple and straight forward programme for adopting a healthier diet and lifestyle to defeat it.   Sadly, Jane died on 4 March 2016, thirty years after her terminal diagnosis and the disease recurring eight times.   She always stuck with her diet and was actually clear of cancer when she passed away from a blood clot.   Jane wrote several books but this one was the first and is a good starting point if you want to read more.

Cancer Free - Your Guide to Gentle, Non-Toxic Healing by Bill Henderson & Carlos M. Garcia MD Bill Henderson watched his late wife Marjorie go through conventional cancer treatment, which destroyed her body in the process of killing her. He made it his mission to help others by researching options that we were ignorant about, and he found over four hundred gentle, non - toxic treatments. Dr Garcia, the co – author, is a traditionally trained M.D. who has broken out of that mould and become a wonderfully informed holistic physician.   He has had great success helping patients with cancer to heal themselves.

The Cancer Revolution by Patricia Peat. With 37 expert contributors, this is your guide integrating complementary and conventional medicine. Patricia Peat spent many years as a nurse working in oncology wards, supporting people through standard treatments – surgery, chemotherapy and radio therapy. She had little interest in Complementary and Alternative Medicine (CAM) until she began to notice that those integrating a range of other therapies into their regime were actually managing better than expected. She became aware of their intense frustration at finding their doctors not only unable and unwilling to engage in constructive dialogue about their options, but unsupportive of their choices. So, in 1998 she set up Cancer Options to support people with cancer in taking charge of their situation, in exploring the widest possible range of treatment options and building in their own integrative treatment programme based around their personal choices. Patricia has helped many of our members at the Cancer Self Help Group Loughborough over the years. She is a medical advisor to Yes to Life and the integrated Healthcare Trust, also a patron of the charity CANCERactive. She is a respected public speaker and writer on the subject of Integrative Medicine and empowering people to make their own health decisions. Her website is https://canceroptions.co.uk/

Yes to Life is a charity which provides information to guide people with cancer through the confusing options for care and lifestyle choices. Their aim is to help them make informed decisions. They simplify the complex and facilitate access to expert knowledge. They also provide financial support in the form of grants for therapies, consultations, nutritional therapy and equipment, all of which help people to manage their condition. Their website is http://yestolife.org.uk/

Do you want to know what we did to Beat Cancer? by Robert Olifent This is the story of Sue Olifent's recovery using natural principles and is a powerful testament for the healing of many types of chronic disease.
Sue and Robert came to talk to our cancer group, and they are truly inspirational. They have a website: www.cancer-acts.com and a Facebook page www.facebook.com/activecancertherapysupport

Breaking Bob the Survival of a Cancer Warrior by Anthony Pillage.   This is a brilliant book written by one of our members who named the massive tumour in his chest 'Bob'. At the age of 53 Anthony Pillage (Pillagius Maximus to his friends) was diagnosed with cancer and given 6 months to live. What started as a sharing of information on social media, especially Facebook, about his illness, soon became a major part of his life.   The love and support that he got from his many friends and followers kept him sane during really bad times and managed to nourish him emotionally and spiritually and helped to keep him going when he felt he could not take any more. So, he decided to write a book based on his Facebook posts.   Breaking Bob is what Tony did best, telling it like it is.   The book is uplifting, hilarious, often scary and a brutally honest account of outwitting cancer.   Sadly, we lost Tony this year, but he outlived his given prognosis and achieved so much following his diagnosis.   He was both inspirational and a real character, larger than life.   We miss him very much but we talk about him most weeks and he has pride of place in our Memories book so he will never be forgotten.
You can get a copy of his book on Amazon or direct from his wife Sarah at sarah@wayofthespiritualwarrior.co.uk

Everything You Need to Know to Help You Beat Cancer by Chris Woollams
Chris is quite probably the leading researcher of cancer in the UK.   Every week research reports on the latest cancer treatments reach his desk from all over the world. Currently editor of the unique magazine 'Integrative Cancer and Oncology News' (Icon) which goes free into over 600 hospitals, health libraries and cancer centres in the UK., he was also founder of CANCER active, now the leading UK cancer charity for integrative, or holistic, cancer treatments and writes on cancer frequently as well as speaking all over the world.
His website is: www.canceractive.com

The Cancer Whisperer by Sophie Sabbage   On learning of her incurable diagnosis, Sophie Sabbage vowed not to be a 'victim'.   Instead, she put herself in charge.   In this ground-breaking book she tells her story and reveals how to cure your fear of cancer, deal with grief, anger and denial, take charge of your treatment and let this illness transform your life.

Last Orders by Patricia Byron This is a book intended to assist anyone and everyone. It was written for my friend Kate and deals with the perennial subject of death. It is not a Will, it is the essential guide to producing your Letter of Wishes and once completed correctly, should save incalculable amounts of stress to those you leave behind, and take most, if not all, of the guesswork out of the administration of your estate. It will offer a vast amount of helpful information about whom your executors should contact, the funeral you wish for, your finances, your belongings and even your pets. I have a copy of this book which I have filled in and I recommend you do the same.

The following books are all about the power of the mind and how your thoughts and beliefs can affect your physiology. The power of the mind is the very crux of this book, it is the one vital element that could make the difference not just to health but to anything and everything in your life. For those of you who like me are sceptics these are books you must read as they provide scientific evidence and proof that everything is possible if you put your mind to it.

The Biology of Belief by Bruce H. Lipton, Ph.D. This book is a must read for those of you that think you are a victim of your genetics -you are not, and Bruce Lipton proves it scientifically in this ground-breaking work in the field of new biology. Author Bruce H. Lipton Ph.D., is a former medical school professor and research scientist. His experiments, and those of other leading-edge scientists, have examined in great detail the mechanisms by which cells receive and process information. The implications of this research radically change our understanding of life. It shows that genes and DNA do not control our biology; but instead, DNA is controlled by signals from outside the cell, including the energetic messages emanating from our positive and negative thoughts. This profoundly hopeful synthesis of the latest research in cell biology and quantum physics is being hailed as a major breakthrough, showing that our bodies can be changed as we retrain our thinking.

Beliefs Pathways to Health and Wellbeing by Robert Dilts, Tim Hallbom &

Suzi Smith. This book offers leading edge technologies that rapidly and effectively identify and remodel limiting beliefs. This manual is unique in that it teaches you powerful processes for change. In it you will learn the latest methods to: Change beliefs which support unhealthy habits such as smoking, overeating and drugs use; change the thinking processes that create phobias and unreasonable fears; retrain your immune system to eliminate allergies and deal optimally with cancer, AIDS, and other diseases; learn how to transform "unhealthy" beliefs into lifelong constructs of wellness.

Energy Medicine Practical Applications and Scientific Proof by C. Norman Shealy, MD, PhD C.Norman Shealy, MD, PhD, is a neurosurgeon, psychologist, and founding president of the American Holistic Medical Association (AHMA). For over three decades he has been at the forefront of alternative medicine and alternative health care. He holds ten patents for innovative discoveries in medicine, has published more than 300 articles and authored more than 24 books. In this complete manual to your health he covers Nutrition and Lifestyle, Mind-Body Medicine, Traditional Chinese medicine, Yoga and Ayurvedic medical systems, Homeopathy, Bioenergetic medicine, Herbal medicine, Dietary supplements and vitamins, Chiropractic and osteopathic therapies and massage. It is a complete manual to health with emphasis on energetic healing approaches for a healthy body.

The Genie in your Genes by Dawson Church Ph.D. We used to think that our DNA determined much of our behaviour as well as our physical characteristics. No more. Exciting new scientific research shows that many genes are being turned on and off - every day - by your beliefs, feelings, and attitudes. Every thought you think ripples throughout your body, affecting your immune system, brain and hormone system. This book - packed with over 300 scientific studies – shows how to take control of your health and wellbeing with thoughts and feelings that raise your level of vitality and happiness.

Mind to Matter is the astonishing science of how your brain creates material reality by Dawson Church. In this book Dawson Church examines the scientific facts and reviews the studies that show, step by step, exactly how our minds create material form. Throughout the book, Dawson Church shares illuminating case histories, up close, authentic, personal accounts of people who had an experience of turning mind into matter.

The Power of your Subconscious Mind by Dr Joseph Murphy. This book is designed to teach you that your habitual thinking and imagery mould, fashion and create your destiny.

Th*e Energy Cure* by William Bengston, PhD - In his early 20s William Bengston received hands-on healing ending his chronic back pain. A self-proclaimed sceptic, he began a 35-year inquiry that made him one of today's leading researchers into the mystery and power of energy medicine. In this book he presents astonishing evidence that challenge us to totally rethink what we believe about our ability to heal. Drawing on his scientific research, incredible results, and mind-bending questions, Bengston invites us to follow him along his 35-year investigation into the mystery of hands-on healing and to discover a technique that may activate your healing abilities.

I have added the next two books to my list of must reads because they contain information that I think it is important for you to know:

It's All in Your Head – the link between mercury amalgams and illness by Dr Hal A. Huggins. Dr Huggins is a dentist, and, in his book, he looks at past research on mercury toxicity and dental amalgams – research that the dental establishment has systematically ignored – and at current scientific findings that can no longer be ignored. It details the link between mercury poisoning and the deteriorating state of the public's health. It describes the possible effects of mercury toxicity, including multiple sclerosis, Alzheimer's disease, Hodgkin's disease, Chronic Fatigue Syndrome, and virtually all autoimmune disorders.

The Great Cholesterol Con – The truth about what really causes heart disease and how to avoid it by Dr Malcolm Kendrick.

Statins are the so-called wonder drugs widely prescribed to lower blood cholesterol levels and claim to offer unparalleled protection against heart disease. Believed to be completely safe and preventing a whole series of other conditions, they are the most profitable drug in the history of medicine. In this ground-breaking book, GP Malcolm Kendrick exposes the truth behind the hype, revealing that high cholesterol levels don't cause heart disease and a high- fat diet – saturated or otherwise - does not affect blood cholesterol levels. The protection provided by statins is so small it is not worth bothering about for most men and all women; statins have many more side effects than has been admitted and their advocates should be treated with scepticism due to their links with drugs' manufacturers. Kendrick lambastes a powerful pharmaceutical industry and unquestioning medical profession, who, he claims, perpetuates the madcap concepts of 'good' and 'bad' cholesterol and cholesterol levels to convince millions of people to spend billions of pounds on statins, thus creating an atmosphere of stress and anxiety – the real cause of fatal heart disease.

The next book was written and compiled by my coach and editor.
A Life on Fire - Bill Ford's Story by Steven Johns MA
In the last year of his life, Bill Ford asked Steve Johns to help him write his memoirs. Bill was a multi-millionaire businessman and had for the last decade of his life run the Great Central Railway as Managing Director (unpaid). Bill had been a Christian Scientist all his life and believed in the principle of Mind over Matter and that you can heal yourself through the power of thought (prayer). He was diagnosed with prostate cancer in the year 2000 when he was 62 years old. He didn't have chemotherapy radiotherapy or surgery, but he did have hormone treatment towards the end of his life in 2018. He lived to see the publication of his book on May 1st, 2018. He died on September 2nd, 2018. If you want to see how far positive thinking can get you - read Bill Ford's story. You will find a link on www.oniontherapy.co.uk to buy a copy of *A Life On Fire*.

Websites

The Truth about Cancer https://go.thetruthaboutcancer.com/
Ty and Charlene Bollinger. This is an excellent website, and you can sign up for their free newsletter here.

Dr Joe Dispensa www.drjoedispensa.com
As a researcher Dr Dispensa's passion can be found at the intersection of the latest findings from the fields of neuroscience, epigenetics and quantum physics, to explore the science behind spontaneous remission. He uses that knowledge to help people heal themselves of illness, chronic conditions and even terminal diseases so that they can enjoy a more fulfilled and happy life.

Kris Carr www.kriscarr.com
Chris has been living with cancer since she was diagnosed with a rare and incurable slow growing stage 1V cancer on Valentine's day in 2003.It taught her so much about taking care of herself and living life to the fullest. The diagnosis sparked a deep desire in her to stop holding back and to start participating in her well-being. Though she can't be cured, she can still be healthy — she can still feel better, love harder and have a more joyful life. So, she hit the road on a self-care pilgrimage and hasn't looked back. More than a decade later, her life is more connected and magical than it was before her diagnosis. Although she still has cancer, she is healthy, and she runs a mission-driven business that serves her community and makes her feel profoundly grateful each and every day. If she can pull that off, just imagine what YOU can do.

Thomas E Levy MD https://www.peakenergy.com/
Dr Thomas E. Levy is a board-certified cardiologist and has written six books on health-related issues. Most of his work has centered on how to restore and maintain good health in the face of the many different forms of toxicity that all of us face, typically on a daily basis.

Ocean Robbins https://www.oceanrobbins.com/
Ocean's grandfather, Irvine Robbins, founded Baskin-Robbins (31 flavours)

ice cream company. Together with his father John Ocean set up the Food Revolution Network.   Food Revolution Network is committed to healthy, ethical, and sustainable food for all. Guided by John and Ocean Robbins, with more than 500,000 members and with the collaboration of many of the top food revolutionary leaders of our times, Food Revolution Network aims to empower individuals, build community, and transform food systems to support healthy people and a healthy planet.
https://foodrevolution.org/

Deepak Chopra   https://www.deepakchopra.com/
Deepak Chopra is an Indian-born American author, public speaker, alternative medicine advocate, and a prominent figure in the New Age movement. Through his books and videos, he has become one of the best-known and wealthiest figures in alternative medicine. He brings together the current research of Western medicine, neuroscience, and physics with the insights of Ayurvedic theory to suggest that the human body is controlled by a "network of intelligence" grounded in quantum reality. He suggests that this intelligence lies deep enough to change the basic patterns that design our physiology.

Louise Hay www.louisehay.com
Through Louise's healing techniques and positive philosophy, millions have learned how to create more of what they want in their lives, including more wellness in their bodies, minds, and spirits. Her own personal philosophy was forged from her tormented upbringing. Her childhood was unstable and impoverished, and her teen years were marked by abuse. Louise ran away from home and ended up in New York City, where she became a model and married a prosperous businessman. Although it appeared that her life had turned around, it was not until the marriage ended 14 years later that her healing really began.

Louise started what would become her life's work in New York City in 1970. She attended meetings at the Church of Religious Science and began training in the ministerial program. She became a popular speaker at the church, and soon found herself counselling clients. This work quickly blossomed into a full-time career. After several years, Louise compiled a reference guide detailing the mental causes of physical ailments and developed positive thought patterns for reversing illness and creating health. This compilation was the basis for Heal Your Body, also known affectionately as "the little blue book." She began traveling throughout the United States, lecturing and facilitating workshops on loving ourselves and healing our lives.   Sadly, Louise died in 2017 at the age of 90.

Dr Tom O'Bryan https://thedr.com/
When it comes to getting healthy Dr Tom O'Bryan's goal for you is "Making It Easy To Do the Right Thing".   As an internationally recognized and compassionate speaker focussing on food sensitivities, environmental toxins, and the development of autoimmune diseases, Dr Tom's audiences discover that it is through a clear understanding of how you got to where you are, that you and your Doctor can figure out what it will take to get you well.   Dr O'Bryan is considered a 'Sherlock Holmes' for chronic disease and teaches that recognising and addressing the underlying mechanisms that activate an immune response is the map to the highway towards better health. He holds teaching Faculty positions with the Institute for Functional Medicine and the National University of Health Sciences.   He has trained and certified tens of thousands of practitioners around the world in advanced understanding of the impact of wheat sensitivity and the development of individual autoimmune diseases.

Dr Ben Nobles Cancer Maps – a diagnostic tool to help doctors understand and apply NICE guidance on recognising and referring cases of suspected cancer.
https://www.gatewayc.org.uk/cancer-maps/

Shulzhenko, Greer, Morgan
https://www.researchgate.net/publication/254263222-bridging_immunity_andlipid_metabolism_by_gut_microbiota

DIETS
The diet that seems to be the one recommended the most for health is the Mediterranean Diet. Here is a link to the NHS website

https://www.nhs.uk/live-well/eat-well/what-is-a-mediterranean-diet/ which explains what it is and how to do it.

Paleo Diet

This diet has become very popular recently. A paleo diet is a dietary plan based on foods similar to what might have been eaten during the Paleolithic era, which dates from approximately 2.5 million to 10,000 years ago.

A paleo diet typically includes lean meats, fish, fruits, vegetables, nuts and seeds — foods that in

the past could be obtained by hunting and gathering. A paleo diet limits food that became

common when farming emerged about 10,000 years ago. These foods include dairy products,

legumes and grains.

Here are a couple of websites, there are many more
https://www.mayoclinic.org/healthy-lifestyle/nutrition-and-healthy-eating/in-depth/paleo-diet/art-20111182
https://www.everydayhealth.com/diet-nutrition/the-paleo-diet.aspx

Plant Based Diet

A plant-based diet is a diet based on foods derived from plants, including vegetables, whole grains, nuts, seeds, legumes and fruits, but with few or no animal products.   Here is a website I found but there are many others

https://www.healthline.com/nutrition/plant-based-diet-guide

The following diets are for those who have health issues and cancer specific diets:

Dr Michael Mosely Lose Weight and reprogram your body.   A scientifically based plan for weight loss and improved blood sugar.   This is a way of life, not just for those at the highest risk of chronic disease, but for anyone who has struggles with their weight and wants to regain control of their health.

https://thebloodsugardiet.com/how-it-works/

Gluten Free Diet: - Coeliac disease is a lifelong autoimmune disease

caused by a reaction to gluten. 1 in 100 people have the condition. Once diagnosed, it is treated by following a gluten free diet for life
https://www.coeliac.org.uk/home/
https://www.mayoclinic.org/healthy-lifestyle/nutrition-and-healthy-eating/in-depth/gluten-free-diet/art-20048530.

The Ketogenic Diet – this is the diet that Dr Patrick Kingsley who worked with us advocated for cancer. It is the diet he recommended for my business partner who chose not to have chemotherapy for his bowel cancer. Despite having lesions in his liver as well as bladder cancer and prostate cancer he is still cancer-free after 6 years. The ketogenic diet is a high fat, adequate protein, low carbohydrate diet that in medicine is used primarily to treat difficult to control epilepsy in children. The diet forces the body to burn fats rather than carbohydrates.

Normally, the carbohydrates contained in food are converted into glucose which is then transported around the body and is particularly important in fuelling brain function However, if little carbohydrate remains in the diet, the liver converts fat into fatty acids and ketone bodies. Ketone bodies pass into the brain and replace glucose as an energy source. An elevated level of ketone bodies in the blood, a state known as ketosis leads to a reduction in the frequency of epileptic seizures. Around half of children and young people with epilepsy who have tried some form of this diet saw the number of seizures drop by at least half, and the effect persists even after discontinuing the diet. Some evidence indicates that adults with epilepsy may benefit from the diet, and that a less strict regimen, such as a modified Atkins diet, is similarly effective.

Here is one website that I found but there are lots more. *https://www.ketofitdiet.co.uk/*

Gerson Therapy: - is probably the best-known alternative approach to cancer treatment.
Gerson Therapy focuses on the role of minerals, enzymes, hormones and other dietary factors in restoring health and wellbeing. It is a natural treatment that boosts your own immune system to heal itself. Drinking

glasses of freshly prepared juices daily, having a vegetarian diet of organically grown fruits and vegetables and eating whole grains are part of the daily regime. Coffee or chamomile enemas are recommended on a regular basis to detoxify the body. Various supplements and enzymes are modified to meet the specific needs of an individual patient.
https://gerson.org/gerpress/

Budwig Diet
Dr Johanna Budwig, the creator of the diet believed that eating a diet very high in polyunsaturated fats would prevent cancer cells from spreading. The diet involves eating multiple servings of a mixture of flaxseed oil and cottage cheese, eating plenty of fresh fruit and vegetables and foods high in fibre, avoiding all processed foods, sugar, butter and margarine and other oils.
https://thetruthaboutcancer.com/budwig-diet-protocol-cancer/

More reading:
Autoimmune Fix by Tom O'Bryan, DC, CCN, DACBN
A Cancer Therapy by Max Gerson M.D
Acupressure Potent Points by Michael Reed Gach
Simple Step-by step Alexander Technique by Michele MacDonnel
Anti Cancer – A new Way of Life by Dr David Servanb-Schreiber
Are You Sleeping in a Safe Place by Rolf Gordon
Beating Cancer with Nutrition by Patrick Quillin PhD RD GNS
The Body Language of Health by Hamish MacGregor
The Bristol Programme by Penny Brohn
Breast Cancer – 50 Essential Things to Do by Greg Anderson
Cancer Is Not a Disease by Andreas Moritz
The Cancer Survivors Companion by Dr Frances Goodhart and Lucy Atkins
The Chemical Maze by Bill Statham
Conventional Cancer Cures – What's the Alternative? by Chris Woollams
The Crystal Handbook by Kevin Sullivan
Feel the Fear and Do it Anyway by Susan Jeffers Ph.D.
The Gerson Therapy by Charlotte Gerson and Morton Walker, P.D.M.
Gut by Guilia Enders
Gut Instinct by Pierre Pallady

Healing Foods by Dr Rosy Daniel
How to Stop Your Doctor Killing You by Vernon Coleman
I believe in Angels by Patricia Wendorf
Juicing for Health by Caroline Wheater
Living Loving and Healing by Bernie Siegal M.D.
The Book of Massage by Lucy Lidell
Mindfulness by Mark Williams and Danny Penman
The Miracle Nutrient Coenzyme Q10 by Emile G. Bliznakov M.D. and Gerald L. Hunt
Miracle of MSM the natural solution for pain by Stanley W. Jacob M.D. Ronald M. Lawrence M.D. Ph.D. and Martin Zucher
Mummy's Lump by Gillian Forest
The Optimum Nutrition Bible by Patrick Holford
The PH Miracle by Robert O. Young Ph.D. and Shelley Redford-Young
Practising Shiatsu by Carola Beresford Cooke
Probiotics and Prebiotics edited by Koen Venema
The Rainbow Diet by Chris Woollams
You Can Heal Your Life by Louise Hay
You Can Conquer Cancer by Ian Gawlor
Stress Buster by Robert Holden
The Field by Lynne McTaggert
The Intention Experiment by Lynne McTaggert
The power of Eight by Lynne McTaggert
Obesity Cancer Depression by F. Batmanghelidgi MD
Your Body's Many Cries for Water by F. Batmanghelidgi MD
Overcoming Binge Eating by Christopher G. Fairburn
How to Stop Smoking and Stay Stopped for Good by Gillian Riley

Support
www.maggiecentres.org excellent source of information and links to support sites for specific cancers
www.youthcancertrust.org support for young people 18-25 and free activity holidays

https://www.pennybrohn.org.uk/.../ge.../courses-national-centre/. Free courses and subsidized retreats for anyone touched by cancer

https://www.roycastle.org/ this is the UK's only Lung Cancer Charity
http://www.prostaid.co.uk/ PROST aid was started in 2006. It is a local, registered charity, based in Wigston Leicestershire. PROST aid covers Leicestershire, Rutland and Northamptonshire. PROST aid receives no government funding and is run by prostate cancer patients, families, friends and urological professionals.

www.beatcancer.org Dr Susan Silberstein PhD how to prevent, cope with and beat cancer through diet, lifestyle and other immune-boosting approaches.

MacMillan Cancer Support - provides physical, emotional and financial support.
  https://www.macmillan.org.uk/
www.mynewhair.org works in partnership with Macmillan Cancer Support to provide advice and information

Marie Curie – supports people living with a terminal illness. They will help you and everyone affected by your diagnosis to achieve the best quality of life. They will support you to keep your independence and dignity for as long as possible
https://www.mariecurie.org.uk/

Together Against Cancer provide help and support for those with cancer
www.togetheragainstcancer.org.uk
Royal Voluntary Service – volunteers offer practical support and share time with older people at home, in hospitals and in the community.
www.royalvoluntaryservice.org.uk
https://www.knittedknockers.org/ The purpose of this website is to help connect volunteer knitters with breast cancer survivors to offer free Knitted Knockers to any woman who wants them.

https://www.nrshealthcare.co.uk/ Low impact pedal exerciser suitable for rehabilitation and gentle exercise. As friction is increased, or during long periods of vigorous exercise, the pedal and housing will become warm to the touch. Not a suitable alternative to a full-size gym exercise bike or similar.

https://www.ncbi.nlm.nih.gov/pmc/articles/PMC3822486/ The work on Telomeres by Nobel prize-winners Elizabeth Blackburn and Carole Greider.

*   *   *

AFTER THOUGHTS and ACKNOWLEDGEMENTS

Well, that's it!   I've done it!   I've written a book!

It has been an amazing journey.   Writing a book is like being on a roller coaster lots of ups and downs, twists and turns, with lots of mixed emotions on the way.   However, my mentor and coach Steve Johns MA was always there to support, encourage, motivate and advise.   Some of the emotions that came up were aspects of events I still needed to deal with and that is when his NLP skills came to the fore, gently steering me through the process of stripping back another layer of the onion. I couldn't have done this without Steve or his wife Mary who, apart from editing, came up with 'peel', 'heal',' reveal' which sums up exactly what Onion Therapy is all about. Thank you both for helping me to make my dream a reality.

So now we have the book what now?

Well, I have another dream, a dream that my book will be a best seller. That will really prove that anyone can do anything if they put their mind to it and believe it despite all the odds. That's where you come in, I need your help. If you like this book and you think it is 'good enough' please tell people about it, share it on social media, Facebook, twitter etc. I want this to get out there, to reach as many people as possible. I want everyone to have the information - information that could prevent them from becoming ill in the first place because there is no doubt about it 'prevention is better than cure'. For those who are already ill then at least they will have information to enable them to take control of their own health and make informed choices about treatment etc.

Just like me, this book is unique. It doesn't fit in. It is not just a self-help book, it is not just a book of resources it is much more than that, it is my life story too and so everyone can benefit from reading it. And if it makes a difference to just one person then writing it will have been worthwhile.

As I said this book is different and so the acknowledgements are going to come at the end instead of the beginning. Here they are: -
I will start with the three people that have made the biggest impact on my life 'Auntie Evelyn' (who died many years ago and who I still miss terribly), Albert Wilde my business partner at CNA and Joyce Walton co-founder of the Cancer Self Help Group Loughborough. Thank you for
believing in me, inspiring and motivating me, and for never giving up on me. I learned so much from you all and I can't put into words how much of an impact you have had on my life. Without you my life would have been very different.

Thank you Leela Mitchelson, if you hadn't said, "I wish you would write this down" when we were talking about the power of the mind at one of the Group meetings, I would never have written the book.

Thank you to all my friends and family, especially my sister Carole who is always there for me and who gave her permission for me to write about our abuse.

Thank you to Mike my partner of 9 years for making my life so much richer, and for putting up with me.

Thank you to all the people I have met in the 10 years that I have been a volunteer at the Cancer Self-Help Group Loughborough. I am so privileged to have met you all. You have shown me what can be achieved if you are determined and believe in yourself. You have taught me not to focus on what you don't have but to focus on what you do. You are a constant reminder that we need to live our lives to the full and treasure every day and I have watched many of you do this and achieve amazing things. I admire, respect and love you all.

For those members who we have lost you will never be forgotten, you touched all of our lives in so many ways and you will always be in our hearts.

Thank you to all the therapists, unpaid volunteers, who give up their valuable time to make sure that all our members have access to complementary therapies which is a very important part of their healing journey, and which means so much to them.

Thank you to Amanda, my friend of 44 years, who I persuaded to be secretary of the Group by telling her it was easy, and she only had to send out one email a week! Fortunately, she believed me.
Thank you, Pete, for agreeing to be Treasurer when no one else would, despite never having done it before. You are both brilliant and you make my job as chairperson seem easy. I couldn't do it without you.

Thank you to all the speakers that also give up their time for free and especially Nasser Butt who not only comes to teach us Tai Chi and much more every month, but he fundraises for us as well. We are so lucky to have one of the best and most knowledgeable instructors, if you don't believe me take a look at his credentials:
http://www.fajing-chuan.co.uk/index.html

Thank you to everyone who has touched my life in the 61 years I have been on this earth, Whether the encounters were good or bad, I am grateful to you all as without you I wouldn't be what I am today. For those of you who hurt me I forgive you, as what I learned from you has contributed to this book one way or another.

Finally thank you to you the reader, for reading this book. I hope that you enjoyed it and that it may prove that you can do anything if you believe it and put your mind to it.

Writing a book was my dream, and with Onion Therapy I made it come true. Your dreams may be different, but the principles are the same. Apply Onion Therapy and you will do it – I promise!
So, what are you waiting for?

The end?

or

Your new beginning…

* * *

FOREWORD by Steven Johns MA
MY STORY Chapter 1
INTRODUCTION BY Paula Reed
INTRODUCTION BY Paula Reed
AFTER THOUGHTS & AKNOWLEDGEMENTS
Then Mother left us, and the angle of the candlelight grew narrower on the wall, and finally went out, closing that day forever.

Laurie Lee - Village Christmas

Jesus Appears to Thomas:
24 Now Thomas, one of the Twelve, was not with the disciples when Jesus came.
25 So the other disciples told him, "We have seen the Lord!"
But he said to them, "Unless I see the nail marks in his hands and put my finger where the nails were, and put my hand into his side, I will not believe."
26 A week later his disciples were in the house again, and Thomas was with them. Though the doors were locked, Jesus came and stood among them and said, "Peace be with you!"
27 Then he said to Thomas, "Put your finger here; see my hands. Reach out your hand and put it into my side. Stop doubting and believe."
28 Thomas said to him, "My Lord and my God!"
29 Then Jesus told him, "Because you have seen me, you have believed; blessed are those who have not seen and yet have believed."

John 20:24-29

"Man is an onion made up of a hundred integuments, a texture made up of many threads. The ancient Asiatics knew this well enough, and in the Buddhist Yoga an exact technique was devised for unmasking the illusion of the personality. The human merry-go-round sees many changes: the illusion that cost India the efforts of thousands of years to unmask is the same illusion that the West has laboured just as hard to maintain and

> strengthen."
>
> Herman Hesse – Steppenwolfe

> "An ounce of prevention is worth a pound of cure."
> — Benjamin Franklin
>
> "My teacher Jim Rohn taught me a simple principle: every day, stand guard at the door of your mind, and you alone decide what thoughts and beliefs you let into your life. For they will shape whether you feel rich or poor, cursed or blessed."
>
> Tony Robbins

Don't Dance So Fast

Have you ever watched kids
On a merry-go-round?
Or listened to the rain
Slapping on the ground?
Ever followed a butterfly's erratic flight?
Or gazed at the sun into the fading night?
You better slow down.
Don't dance so fast.
Time is short.
The music won't last.

Do you run through each day
On the fly?
When you ask "How are you?"
Do you hear the reply?
When the day is done
Do you lie in your bed
With the next hundred chores
Running through your head?
You'd better slow down
Don't dance so fast.
Time is short.

The music won't last.

Ever told your child,
We'll do it tomorrow?
And in your haste,
Not see his sorrow?
Ever lost touch,
Let a good friendship die
Cause you never had time
To call and say "Hi"?
You'd better slow down.
Don't dance so fast.
Time is short.
The music won't last.

When you run so fast to get somewhere
You miss half the fun of getting there.
When you worry and hurry through your day,
It is like an unopened gift....
Thrown away.
Life is not a race.
Do take it slower
Hear the music Before the song is over.

Author Unknown

The Lady With The Lamp
(Saint Filomena)

Whene'er a noble deed is wrought
Whene'er is spoken a noble thought
Our hearts, in glad surprise,
To higher levels rise.

The tidal wave of deeper souls
Into our inmost being rolls,
And lifts us unawares

Out of all meaner cares.

*Honour to those whose words or deeds
Thus help us in our daily needs,
And by their overflow
Raise us from what is low!*

*Thus thought I, as by night I read
Of all the great army of the dead,
The trenches cold and damp,
The starved and frozen camp,*

*The wounded from the battle-plain
In dreary hospitals of pain,
The cheerless corridors,
The cold and stony floors.*

*Lo! in that house of misery
A lady with a lamp I see
Pass through the glimmering of gloom
And flit from room to room.*

*And slow, as in a dream of bliss,
The speechless sufferer turns to kiss
Her shadow, as it falls
Upon the darkening walls.*

*As if a door in heaven should be
Opened, and then closed suddenly,
The vision came and went,
The light shone and was spent.*

*On England's annals, through the long
Hereafter of her speech and song,
That light its rays shall cast
From portals of the past.*

> A lady with a lamp shall stand
> In the great history of the land,
>   A noble type of good,
>   Heroic womanhood.
>
> Nor even shall be wanting here
> The palm, the lily, and the spear,
>   The symbols that of yore
>   Saint Filomena bore.

Henry Wadsworth Longfellow

A Song of Living

Because I have loved life, I shall have no sorrow to die.
I have sent up my gladness on wings, to be lost in the blue of the sky.
I have run and leaped with the rain, I have taken the wind to my breast.
My cheeks like a drowsy child to the face of the earth I have pressed.
Because I have loved life, I shall have no sorrow to die.

I have kissed young love on the lips, I have heard his song to the end,
I have struck my hand like a seal in the loyal hand of a friend.
I have known the peace of heaven, the comfort of work done well.
I have longed for death in the darkness and risen alive out of hell.
Because I have loved life, I shall have no sorrow to die.

I gave a share of my soul to the world, when and where my course is run.
I know that another shall finish the task I surely must leave undone.
I know that no flower, nor flint was in vain on the path I trod.
As one looks on a face through a window, through life I have looked on God,
Because I have loved life, I shall have no sorrow to die.

Amelia Josephine Burr

A

A Modern Version of the Hippocratic Oath

I swear to fulfil, to the best of my ability and judgment, this covenant:

I will respect the hard-won scientific gains of those physicians in whose steps I walk, and gladly share such knowledge as is mine with those who are to follow.

I will apply, for the benefit of the sick, all measures which are required, avoiding those twin traps of overtreatment and therapeutic nihilism.

I will remember that there is art to medicine as well as science, and that warmth, sympathy, and understanding may outweigh the surgeon's knife or the chemist's drug.

I will not be ashamed to say "I know not," nor will I fail to call in my colleagues when the skills of another are needed for a patient's recovery.

I will respect the privacy of my patients, for their problems are not disclosed to me that the world may know.

Most especially must I tread with care in matters of life and death. If it is given me to save a life, all thanks. But it may also be within my power to take a life; this awesome responsibility must be faced with great humbleness and awareness of my own frailty. Above all, I must not play at God.

I will remember that I do not treat a fever chart, a cancerous growth, but a sick human being, whose illness may affect the person's family and economic stability. My responsibility includes these related problems, if I am to care adequately for the sick.

I will prevent disease whenever I can, for prevention is preferable to cure.

I will remember that I remain a member of society, with special obligations to all my fellow human beings, those sound of mind and body as well as the infirm.

If I do not violate this oath, may I enjoy life and art, respected while I live and remembered with affection thereafter.

May I always act so as to preserve the finest traditions of my calling and may I long experience the joy of healing those who seek my help.

The modern version of the Hippocratic Oath was written in 1964 by Louis Lasagna, Dean of the School of Medicine at Tufts University.

Knowledge

Now that I know
That passion warms little
Of flesh in the mold,
And treasure is brittle,

I'll lie here and learn
How, over their ground,
Trees make a long shadow
And a light sound.

by Louise Bogan

Printed in Great Britain
by Amazon

64704922R00098